Perturbation

Perturbation

A Speculative History of Future(s) Past

Rouzbeh Akhbari

Designed by David Schnitman

In memory of my late grandfather, Mahmoud Dehnavi, whose inspiring imagination continues to captivate many to this day.

Contents

....

The idea behind the following stories came about when I revisited my maternal grandmother's home in Isfahan, Iran, after being away for eight years. The main reason behind my initial departure was to avoid conscription as a young adult. I had other reasons too, of course. I come from a strangely political family. My grandfather was tortured and imprisoned for being a socialist Toudeh supporter, and my father for being an intelligence officer serving the Shah's pro-western regime. Coupled with my own background of high school expulsions on more than one occasion, little hope remained for me to be admitted into university. Things began to look a little more promising when the 2009 post-election 'Green Revolution' erupted, but those uprisings were swiftly subdued, leaving me no choice but to immigrate and start afresh somewhere else. The journey initially took me to Kuala Lumpur, later across Syria, and finally to Canada; places I never even anticipated I would visit during my lifetime.

My return to Isfahan after all these years was quite memorable in many respects, yet, every time I recall that trip, the first thing that comes to mind is a portfolio that I found in my late grandfather Mahmoud Dehnavi's studio. After his passing in 2001, my grandmother lived in their old adobe bungalow in solitude. Despite her deteriorating physical abilities, she put meticulous care into keeping baba Mahmoud's basement studio spotless. I serendipitously found the leather-wrapped portfolio shoved haphazardly in his bookshelf between the over-sized *Tabari History* volumes. The illustrations were extremely elaborate, yet embodied an aura that made me feel as if he had weaved it together, like a refreshing breeze hugging the leaves of a willow tree on a hot summer's day. A dozen of his handwritten notes were in the bundle too. Most of them were calligraphic reproductions of couplets by the prominent poet, Hafiz. A few, however, looked like annotations from archeological textbooks about Portuguese forts in the

Persian Gulf and Isfahani Safavid Gardens.

Curious to know more, I begged my grandmother to tell me all she knew about the illustrations and why they had never been publicized. She didn't remember much but was able to confirm that they were produced sometime between 1974 and 1984, when Baba Mahmoud worked on projects for the court of Sultan Qaboos in Oman. She specifically mentioned that he became obsessed with desert agriculture and imperial gardens while working remotely in Khasab and Qeshm. As to my question about why they were kept hidden until now, she was suspiciously uninterested and simply brushed them aside as "unfinished," claiming he had much better masterpieces for people to enjoy!

Since that hot August day four years ago, these drawings have become my *Zahir*. I was thirsty for information and no one in the family had anything to offer. Finally, I embraced the challenge and embarked on a journey to explore the geopolitical context and mythological dimensions of this fascinating find. The research quickly spiraled into a wild set of new narratives that took me to numerous historical archives between Lisbon, Doha, London, Isfahan, and Bandar Abbas. Navigating these records accentuated the intertwined relations between the serpentine history of the greater Hormuz region and its connection to the evolution of unique teleological, cosmic and planetary sociopolitical thoughts.

Through multiple conversations with my father, I was able to take inspiration from his insider technical and historical knowledge as a linguist intelligence officer whose primary role in the SAVAK[1] was to analyze the links between a wide array of religious revolutionaries and foreign organizations; particularly, emerging movements in western Europe and those in polities under the Soviets' sphere of influence. My month-long fieldwork between Isfahan and Hormuz played a crucial role in the development of this work; alas, the process came to an abrupt closure due to the military confrontations between the US and Iran, which led to the tragic murder of 176 passengers aboard Ukrainian Airlines PS752 by the Islamic Revolutionary Guard Corps (IRGC) on January 8, 2020. Throughout the research and development process, I met many generous souls who blessed me with their mere existence, inspirations, and stories. Some of these individuals and narratives found their way directly into the following chapters, while others formed the shoulders upon which my fictional characters stand.

---

1   Sazman Amniat va Etelaate Keshvar (National Security and Intelligence Organization).

The strait of Hormuz today has an extremely complex socioeconomic and political fabric that sees local and transnational actors engage in intelligence collection, informal commodity exchange, arms trafficking, and ongoing acts of infrastructural and military sabotage. A handful of these actors have grown to be my close friends, while most chose to keep distant. It goes without saying that all the names and identifying factors in the following pages have been carefully obscured to assure the safety of everyone whose livelihood is entangled with the contemporary struggles surrounding this narrow waterway.

Lastly, to contextualize the following stories and ease you into what might initially feel like a series of disjointed events, I'll briefly elaborate on the book's title. In astrophysics, 'perturbation' is used to refer to the complex motion of a massive body subjected to forces other than the gravitational attraction of a single other body. The additional forces can include a third (or fourth, fifth, etc.) external body, internal resistance, or the off-center attraction of an oblate or otherwise misshapen body. Keeping in mind this definition, both for its literal meaning and as a metaphor will be helpful in grasping the characters' relations to the macro events described in the upcoming pages.

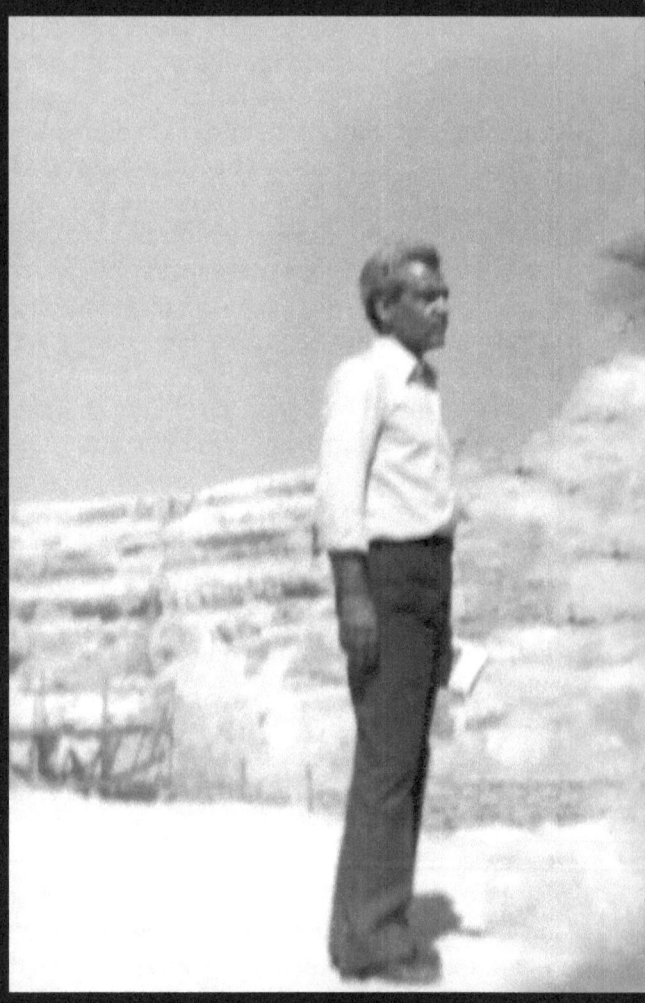

M. DEHNAVI, CIRCA 1979, GIZA

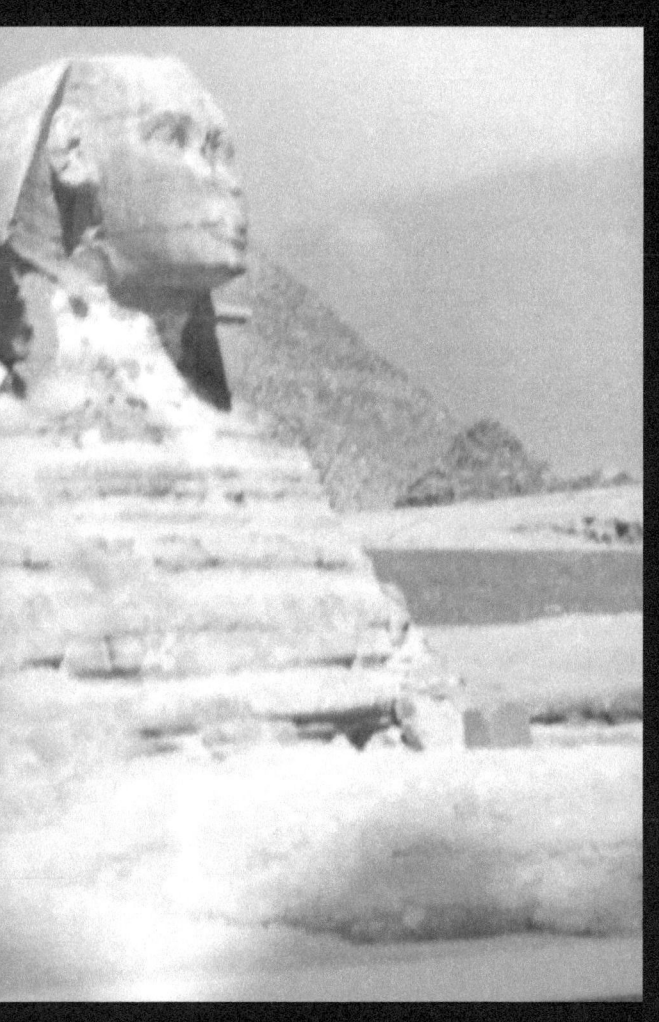

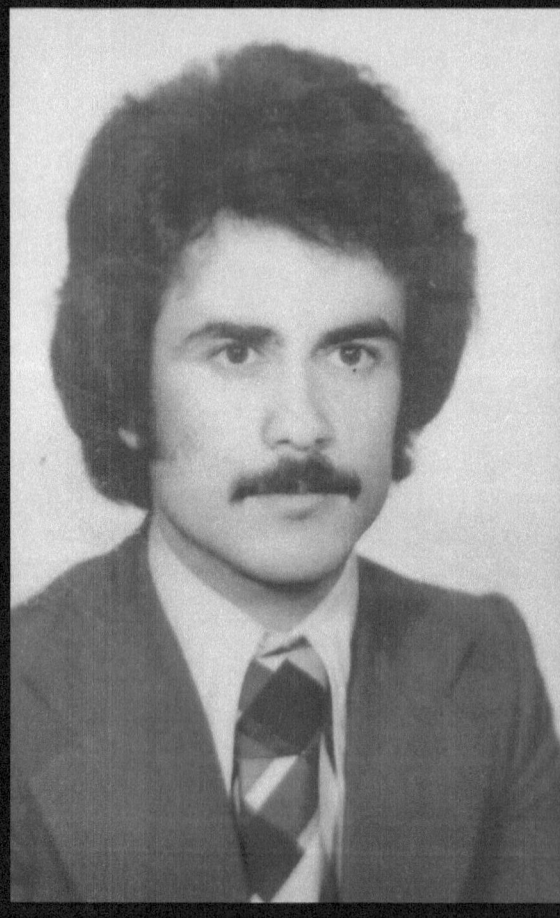

M. H. AKHBARI, 1979, TEHRAN

CHAPTER ONE

On Revolution(s) Past

Diogo's status was one of great honor in the public eye. Not only was he showered in fame for being remarkably skilled at his job, but also widely trusted across the nation as an honest man; so much so that the King, along with his most experienced sailors trusted his judgment more than their own. As the royal certifier of all compass needles amended across the realms of Philip IV, his title carried great political power. A growing population who relied on the ocean as their medium of exchange, including cartographers, merchants, insurance underwriters, and navy servicemen bargained for the secrets of his trade. Over two decades of service amongst the King's closest circles brought him a massive fortune in gold, properties and livestock. It would be an overstatement to say his life was all privilege, though.

His key position in the function of the vast imperial fleet brought him many enemies, among whom Admiral Álvaro Botelho was the most vicious. Botelho was a devout Christian whose ancestors came to prominence in the early 1400s by fighting against the Moorish occupation. Their long-standing feud was ignited six years earlier when Diogo refused to certify Botelho's reinforcement carracks in time for sailing towards Comorão. The delay caused Botelho's fleet vital time as the seasonal easterlies subsided and rendered the seas impossible to navigate for the remainder of that year. Although widely celebrated by the King, insurers, soldiers and the armada's lower ranked sailors, Diogo's decision resulted in the humiliating defeat of the besieged forces in Asia whose wishes of receiving military support from the metropole were never granted.

Over the next years, Botelho tried to undermine Diogo's work time and time again by filing false reports of malfunctions in the compasses certified by him. During his return voyages from eastern territories, Botelho used to bribe the dock workers in the *feitorias* [2] along the coasts of Aden and Socotra to sneak into incoming vessels and selectively demagnetize the compass needles. They did so by adding a salt and lime juice concoction to the base leveling liquid used inside their navigational barrels. Of course, Botelho never informed the poor dockers about the torturous punishments that King Philip IV had set out for anyone tampering with the needles certified by his court. The systemic sabotage carried out by those longshoremen resulted in the disappearance of nine cargo ships loaded with valuable ceramics and spices during the early months of 1621. On top of these losses, thirty-two ships made it back to Europe with significant delays, depleted food sources, and a handful of cannibals—that is, among the seamen fortunate enough to survive. This caused an uproar amongst the sailors and businessmen alike. By May of the same year, the crowded pubs lining the alleys leading to the docklands in Faro and Lisbon became sites of violent outbreaks between the seafarers and the sovereign. The damages caused by the shadow of doubt cast over Diogo's accuracy wasn't just limited to these uprisings, however. The most destabilizing aspect of the situation was the skyrocketing navigation fees that merchants and ship owners had to absorb into their operating costs, and by

---

2   Factory. Common name for a Medieval entrepot: an early form of free trade zone.

extension, pass onto the consumers. Even if the skilled traders managed to find an experienced navigator to steer their vessel, it was next to impossible to convince competent assistants to join the long expeditions across the globe with such levels of uncertainty. Under these circumstances, more and more shipmasters turned to deception in order to staff their vessels. Intoxicated sailors frequenting the watering holes adjacent to the Tagus River were the perfect targets for the departing skippers, who tricked the hapless drunkards into boarding the ships, effectively kidnapping them with no means of return when they woke up onboard the next day.

Within just a few months, the chaos became so severe that the King had no choice but to intercept the markets to stop the price hikes and penalize the opportunist gougers. Subsequently, he ordered Diogo arrested and his assets confiscated. With the intention of quenching the flames of an ongoing sailors' revolt, he arranged for Diogo to be tried in public and set aflame near the gates of the crowded fish market in Belem.

Confident in the quality of his workmanship, Diogo categorically refused to plead guilty in the weeks prior to his tribunal. He insisted that the errors had originated abroad. Exerting his little remaining political influence, he was able to plant the seeds of mercy in the King's mind by provoking his paranoia and suggesting that the Ottoman rivals had been actively sabotaging his vast maritime infrastructure. Out of pure luck, a trusted witch interpreted the King's disturbing dream a fortnight before the trial in Diogo's favor, too. In that dream, Philip IV had seen himself stranded in a lush oasis in the middle of a vast desert with nothing but a simple wooden kamal and a handful of rusty nails, none of which he knew how to utilize for navigational purposes. Gravely dehydrated and unable to find his way out of the dunes, he observed the soul leave his body while hyenas, vultures, and worms feasted on his flesh. Distraught by those visions, he summoned Axera, the court's most talented storyteller, to solicit her advice. Upon hearing a detailed account of the King's nightmare, she let out a sigh and exclaimed, "Such woes! The ground shifts beneath your feet. Stars are abandoning the skies and your enemies remain eternally joyful. I assure you that the compass betrays you not, your grace! It is the vast marble itself that plays these tricks on your needles."

Just as easily convinced of Diogo's innocence as he was of his guilt, the King ordered him acquitted at once and installed as the head of a taskforce to investigate the anomalies along the trade routes between the Iberian and Arabian peninsulas. He was offered a large accompanying armada and given a decree to severely punish anyone who was found guilty of tampering with the king's magnets. Since Diogo had no family for the King to take hostage as he embarked on the journey, his vast riches and properties were to remain confiscated as to ensure his return. Fearing that the eye-catching carracks could bring unnecessary spectacle to the investigation and potentially tip off the criminals before his arrival, Diogo chose to depart aboard the Escorpião, an old but sleek cargo caravel owned by his distant cousin.

He insisted on keeping the mission a secret in public and carefully hired a small crew of six trusted sailors to accompany him. With the hopes of taking timely advantage of the lifting westerlies, they left the harbor under the cover of night on August 9, 1621. Initially, the gossip of their departure didn't circulate too much, but Botelho was eventually tipped off by his dock-worker accomplices who suspected the true purpose of the Escorpião's expedition after noticing it left with an empty cargo hall except a few barrels of metal shavings, four crow-filled birdcages, and a couple of chests stuffed with various ephemerides. Terrified at the prospect of the truth being revealed, Botelho had no

choice but to desert his ranks and flee to Ana-
tolia with the hopes of recruiting competent
Ottoman mercenaries to intercept the Escorpião
at high seas. With the help of his wife's falsifica-
tions, he managed to unroll the perfect coverup
scenario to make his absence come across as an
abduction by enemy scouts while on duty in a
trading post near Tangiers.

Meanwhile, the expedition was well under-
way as the Escorpião's crew randomly stopped
to inspect compasses at different feitorias
along the maritime route to Goa. To ensure that
the magnets aboard their vessel were always
accurate, Diogo used his portable distillation
device and iron shavings to create a new compass every single day. In the earlier stages of
their investigations, which included all the ports
to the west and north of the Cape of Good Hope,
it became clear that all the faulty needles were
aboard ships making the westward voyage back
to Europe. To the east of this point, however,
in addition to the oceanic voyageurs, some of
the vessels engaged in regional trade were also
affected. It so happened that the largest number of ships vanished in this part of the Indian
Ocean, too. While gathering testimonies from
the locals, the widows of disappeared seamen
from the coasts of Sofala and Moputo were
particularly sorrowful, begging Diogo and his

colleagues to locate their missing lovers. Judging from the evidence gathered, they deduced that the source of all troubles must be somewhere between the tip of India and the Sea of Oman, with Ormuz being the most probable candidate due to its well-known anti-Portuguese sentiments. With the clarity emerged from those inquiries, they now had a precise destination to sail to; however, a major obstacle quickly arose. The subsiding winds and reversing oceanic currents made it dangerous for the caravel to continue the journey northward. Sueira, the expedition's well-travelled skipper, proposed two alternative plans involving three months of idling either in the ports of Muscat, or Aden. Diogo wasn't particularly opinionated on this subject, so the deck boss and his rigging assistant, Pero, took the lead in making the decision on their behalf. Pero claimed that one of his well-to-do childhood friends, who was posted to manage the salt feitoria in Aden, would make an ideal host during their repose. Thus, in pursuit of comfortable beds and home-cooked meals, they sailed upon rapidly reversing gyres and passed the horn of Africa towards Bab-Al Mandab.

According to historical port logs, their caravel anchored just north of the Sirah Fortress on the morning of March 2, 1622. Upon arrival, all the crew members except Sueiro and Diogo disembarked and magically disappeared among the crowds unloading the end-of-season cargo from China. While Diogo locked his extensive wind roses inside a large chest in the upper deck next to the fore-staffs and quadrants, Sueiro tidied up the ropes, fed the leftover grains from the previous night's supper to the crows and covered their cages with a wet burlap. Before disembarking, Diogo packed his royal decree under his capote next to the poisonous dagger that he habitually carried around. Once ashore, the sublimity of the splendid hills covered in fortifications stretching all the way to the jetty was replaced by the nauseating smell of rotten fish heads and shrimps that were drying under the sun. Fleeing the stench, they followed the first corridor that led away from the main square. Having no clue about the whereabouts of the feitoria that Pero mentioned earlier, they wandered the labyrinthine medina in search of their shipmates.

Exhausted from the futile quest in the heat, they reluctantly climbed a hill overlooking the city's infamous crater in search of a better vantage point. By the time they were on top, Aden's soundscape was saturated with men yelling the *Azaan*[3] from what sounded like hundreds of rooftops. Sueira pulled out his binoculars when they were high enough to see the jetty again. As soon as he focused the lens on the now-quiet port lands, he noticed two strangers rummaging about aboard the Escorpião. He immediately alarmed Diogo and charged down the hill like a wild cat. Middle-aged Diogo followed suit but the poor man was much less agile. By the time he arrived at the embarkation ladder, Sueira was already on the upper deck, grappling with one of the intruders. The moment Diogo made it onboard, a sickle-wielding man whose face was covered with a blue scarf attacked him. In a quick maneuver, Diogo managed to insert his sharp dagger deep into the man's chest, puncturing his lung. Gasping for air, his victim fell onto the unlucky crows and crushed the wooden cages under his weight. Making his way across the vessel, Diogo quietly sneaked behind the second intruder who was suffocating Sueira with his bare hands, and shoved the virulent dagger into his neck. It was only a matter of seconds before the prowler lay lifeless on the deck.

It took Sueira a few minutes to regain his composure. Assuming the trespassers were random burglars scavenging their empty cargo hall,

---

3   Islamic daily call to prayer.

they decided to split up and inspect the vessel for damages or theft. Diogo searched the orlop, while Sueira continued to inspect the steering deck. To his utmost surprise, Diogo was confronted with Pero's severely wounded body abandoned inside the cargo hall. The thumb and index fingers on his right hand were severed, and his face was swollen from what looked like multiple fractures on his skull. Together they managed to relocate Pero into the sleeping quarters and cleanse his wounds. As they struggled to postulate what happened to the rest of the crew, Diogo noticed that the man he had stabbed earlier was no longer on the deck. They both hurried out of the cabin and were instantly confronted with a terrifying sight that ran a cold shiver down their spines.

Hordes of angry sword-yielding locals were racing towards the jetty. As the pack closed in, their overpowering war cries froze Diogo and Sueira in their places. By the time they curbed the daze and managed to react, the mob was already about fifty yards away. Diogo hastily cut off the anchor ropes while Sueira climbed the mast like a monkey and unfurled the mainsail. A huge gust filled the fabric immediately. After a sudden jolt followed by loud creaking noises, the ship began its gradual movement. In the absence of the steering jib which rendered the helm inoperational, the vessel was rapidly heeling; pushing the bow against the jetty as the stern rotated around a perpendicular axis. Although the embarkation ladder was already distant from the dock, a couple of raiders jumped into the water and swam towards the ship while the rest threw spears at the steering deck. Having no option but to unfurl the jib, Sueira cautiously sneaked to the front, mounted the boom, and pulled vigorously on the release lines. The sail that was unresponsive at first suddenly filled with wind and aggressively threw the boom starboard, quickly stabilizing the heeling caravel. Since the mob's projectiles pinned Diogo in the back of the vessel, no one was present to tie the jib's lines and stop the boom from drifting aimlessly. Just as the ship was gaining speed and departing the jetty's narrow exit, a violent shake caused by a collision with a small rowboat launched ill-fated Sueira, who was struggling on the wobbly boom, overboard. By the time Diogo realized what had happened, the Escorpião was hundreds of yards away from the jetty and Sueiro had already faced his wretched death at the hands of the angry crowd.

Considering the unfavorable sailing conditions at that time of year, and the fact that he now had to captain the vessel all by himself, Diogo decided to keep the Escorpião as close to the shoreline as possible. For a while, his efforts maintained the ship relatively on track but the seasonal gyres were sure to pull him deep into the ocean if he deviated ever so slightly. In the first week, his time was split between deck chores, tending to Pero's wounds, and carefully recording the vessel's exact position.

After regaining his consciousness, Pero recounted the events leading to their brutal encounter with the Adenes. Apparently, as soon as they disembarked, the crew befriended a group of dock workers who invited them for beers in a local pub near the salt feitoria. During a stuporous rant after an hour of heavy drinking, Pero accidentally revealed the real intention of their mission, and soon after, a group of unknown men arrived at the pub, kidnapped and tortured all of them until they revealed the whereabouts of their anchorage point. Hoping to find the rest of the crew onboard, they forced Pero back onto the ship as a hostage and the fatal encounters at the jetty ensued.

In the absence of effective medication, Pero's health, which had been stabilizing at first, deteriorated quickly. On the eleventh day after leaving Aden, he fell ill with a severe fever and died shortly after from septic shock. Later that day, with little remaining morale as the last living soul on that caravel, Diogo sat on the upper deck in solitude to watch the sunset. A thin cloud was forming near the horizon, making the magical scenery even more resplendent. Lost in the vista's magnificence, he noticed the silhouette of a distant vessel about fifty degrees south. At first, he suspected that his eyes were burnt from staring into the sun, but the ship seemed to become ever clearer as moments passed. Using a powerful set of binoculars that he found in Sueiro's room, he scrutinized the incoming vessel and found out in great horror that it was hovering above the horizon. The ship was not touching the sea at all! Of course, any sailor with experience in these latitudes would have known that the spectral fata morgana was a common sighting when wind currents pushed the colder air close to the surface, but in a state of panic, Diogo steered away from the approaching vessel as the night fell.

It was a particularly dark, moonless evening. Fearing that a satanic ghost ship was in pursuit, he put out the lights, threw all the reflective materials overboard, and hid inside the orlop. After a few hours of praying in solitude, he was convinced that the devil's ship had left his vicinity, and gathered the courage to go up on the main deck again. As soon as he sneaked his head out, a row of bright flashes followed by thunderous explosions filled the sky. In an instant, heavy cannonballs were landing in the waters next to him. When he managed to peek at the assaulting vessel illuminated by the roaring cannon fire, he realized that it was a gigantic multi-sail Turkish galleon. Knowing that the Escorpião stood no chance against such a beast, he tried to exploit the caravel's only advantage: its agility. He ran for the mast and tightened all the lines to unroll the sail at full length. The heavy gusts filled the mainsail, advancing the ship full speed ahead. Once at the helm, he rapidly drifted the boom all the way starboard, causing the lifting winds to fill the jib too. Rotating counterclockwise, the Escorpião heeled drastically and headed straight towards the galleon. Thus far, all cannonballs had missed, and Diogo's sudden maneuver was making it even more difficult for his opponents to take aim. As he charged towards the galleon with increasing speed, a cannonball struck the vessel's bow at a sharp angle and destroyed Notus'[4] statue that was fitted on the vessel as a figurehead. A subsequent explosion dispersed multiple pieces of shrapnel on the side of the main haul, causing the rushing water to fill the ballast tanks which somewhat balanced the excessive heeling. Noting the Escorpião's direct collision course, Bekir

---

4   Notus (Nótos) was the Greek God of the south wind.

Pasha, the galleon's captain, ordered a swift clockwise maneuver to clear the path and aim the galleon's stern at the caravel to hunt it at point-blank. Alas, the galleon's sluggish action sealed its miserable fate. By the time the giant managed to turn around, the caravel's well-reinforced bow struck the galleon's massive rudder. In turn, the unmounted rudder crashed onto the Escorpião's stern and completely demolished the steering room, upper decks, and sleeping quarters, sinking all of Diogo's essential navigational tools and ephemerides. The accident was strong enough to delaminate the jib and make the primary mast slightly crooked as well. Continuing onwards, the Escorpião left the scene as hundreds of sailors aboard the galleon rushed to adjust the sails to prevent their vessel from entering a deadly spin and tipping over. As the cannon fire stopped and their distance grew, the night's darkness embraced both vessels again.

Despite getting out of the dreadful altercation alive, Diogo's chances of survival were now very slim. Not only did he lose the distillation device and all his navigational tools, but the caravel was critically damaged too. He had abundant food and drinkable liquids onboard, however, without his accurate watch and ephemerides, celestial navigation was next to impossible. His inability to calculate travel direction and speed, especially in that perilous part of the Indian Ocean, meant that little beside luck could bring him back to land.

From then on, he embraced a strict routine and relied solely on Polaris' fixed position to find his way. The jib's absence, along with the mainsail's severe condition, made his journey much slower than usual. In order to calculate his speed without a clock, he invented a new time unit by boring a tiny hole at the bottom of a wooden cup, floating it on a tub of water and designating the duration that it took to sink as a single unit of time. The cup had interior markings which he utilized to measure shorter periods of time as fractions of a full cup. To calculate his speed in different sailing conditions, he stood at the vessel's bow, dropped a woodchip into the sea, and measured how long it took for it to pass parallel to the stern using his newly invented time unit. These methods seemed to work well for the first three weeks, but as time passed, the Northern Star became fainter and fainter to the naked eye. At first, Diogo assumed that his eyesight was deteriorating due to malnutrition and continued exposure to the elements, but soon he realized that his eyes had no problem registering the light from other celestial bodies at all. The strange phenomenon continued until Polaris was completely undetectable.

Having lost the only constant in the night' sky, he could only rely on the sun's position and his rudimentary speedometer from then on. On two occasions, he felt a vague intuition that a land-mass might be near and optimistically released one of the crows. In both instances the bird flew aimlessly for a short while, hovered above the vessel, and finally landed back on the deck. Convinced that the gyres were pushing him along a circle in the middle of the ocean, he slowly lost all hope for a rescue and gave up on registering the ship's estimated position every day. Instead, he spent most of his days staring at the crows that were by then roaming freely on the deck.

One afternoon, he noticed a crow fly away, but he dismissed it as yet another pointless fly-by. He was falling in and out of sleep at random those days, and soon after the bird's departure, he also dozed off. After waking up near sun-set and seeing no sign of the crows, Diogo was ecstatic. He was convinced that the birds had found another surface to land on. Since nothing was visible from the deck, he excitedly climbed the warped mast and carefully inspected the horizon; but he found nothing, nothing at all. Just as he was climbing back down more hope-lessly than ever, he caught sight of a small grain barge that was stuck to the demolished stern and being dragged by the Escorpião. He hastily ran to the back and saw the crows feasting on the grains aboard the barge. The small vessel was attached precariously with a relatively thin rope to the broken beams that used to hold up the upper deck. Fearing that he might lose the precious crows to the grains, he picked up a large wicker basket, tied a sturdy line around his waist and descended onto the barge. As he was desperately trying to catch the birds one by one, he came across a baby carriage left under the barge's sunshade. He approached it slowly, lifted the thin covers and astoundingly found a toddler sleeping calmly inside! While he stared in disbelief, the screeching noises from the beams that were holding onto the barge got louder and more noticeable. Fearing an imminent collapse, he hastily picked up the child and climbed back onto the Escorpião. Awakened by the sudden shakes and noises, the child cried loudly.

Once on the deck, Diogo prepared a bowl of coconut-soaked oats for the child, but he was disinterested in the meal and kept crying for hours until he fell asleep. Not knowing what to do, Diogo also closed his eyes and soon dozed off too. Hours later, a crack of lightning woke him up in the middle of the night as a thunderous monsoon approached from the east. Concerned that the heavy winds might rip the fabric, he got up to lower the mainsail. The child, however, was gone. Initially, there was no sign of him at all, but Diogo eventually found him on the upper deck and shockingly stared as the toddler single-handedly pulled down the sails, ordered the lines, and tightened the pulleys that had become undone during the collision with the galleon. Once the child was done, he sat silently on the floor and pointed to the entrance of the orlop deck, where Diogo took refuge for the remainder of that evening to weather the storm.

Believing the child to be a Godsent savior, Diogo carefully watched all his actions. However, no matter how hard he tried to decode his every move, the child screamed until he was left alone. Every time a pair of eyes laid upon him, even those of the crows, the child would object by crying loudly for hours. Giving up on the hopes of learning anything special from him, Diogo let the toddler roam onboard without paying him much attention. Having no contact with humans for more than four months had already brought him to the verge of madness, and the lack of any foreseeable rescue was making it even worse. He no longer did any deck chores or cared to look at the stars or the sun's position, which in turn pushed him even deeper into the abyss of despair and depression. Although he still had enough food to continue for another two months, he barely ate at all and was becoming more frail day by day.

Laying on a wicker mat and waiting to embrace his somber fate after an unknown number of days had passed, Diogo heard a loud roar from the ship's bow followed by an aggressive jolt. When he gathered the strength to get to his feet and inspect the surroundings, he realized that the Escorpião had run aground on a sandy shore. The impact was forceful enough for the mainsail's mighty mast to collapse. The sight brought tears of joy to his eyes and gave him a sudden rush of energy. Screaming euphorically, he searched the deck for the child and found him near the bow as he silently played with the woodchips that were strewn around after the incident. Strangely enough, the child wasn't at all bothered by Diogo's gaze this time.

Once ashore, Diogo was so delighted at the sensation of walking on solid ground that all the weakness from months of malnutrition seemed to disappear in an instant. The shoreline and its shimmering hues looked astonishing under the spotless blue sky. Despite the sparse vegetation on the island, multilayers of colorful sediments on the surrounding hills gave it a lively atmosphere. It was around noon and the extreme sunshine scorching the soil was impeding Diogo's efforts to move away from the shipwreck. After only a few yards of walking, he noticed three horsemen and a dozen individuals on foot charging towards the beach. Fearing an encounter similar to that of the Adenes, he embraced the child firmly and fled towards the closest hills. In the absence of any shrubs to take cover in, he struggled to wedge himself into a cave-like opening at the bottom of a silvery salt rock.

Peeking from an ideal vantage point inside the cave, he saw no sign of the horsemen. The crowds on foot were carefully inspecting the shipwreck, but the horsemen were nowhere to be seen. Just as he was about to let out a sigh of relief, a black horse bent its neck and sniffed the air inside the cave. A short man jumped off, pulled out his sabre, and walked to the narrow entrance while the horse licked the gigantic salt rock. He glanced inside the cave and yelled for his companions' assistance to pull Diogo and the poor child out of the hole. Pressing the tip of his sword against Diogo's throat, the man demanded him to identify himself in fluent Portuguese. Ecstatic at hearing the soldier's voice and realizing he was back in the realms of King Philip IV, he revealed his royal decree and offered a brief explanation of everything that had taken place since they left Lisbon. The gist of his narrative arose little suspicion but the toddler's presence, who was surprisingly quiet during this interaction, made it difficult for them to believe the details. They thus arrested him so that the island's viceroy could make the final verdict on his case.

As they were relocating Diogo and the child to the vaults beneath the fort of Our Lady of Conception, the serpentine pathways among vibrantly colored hills gave way to an open vista overlooking the docklands. Diogo had never seen such overcrowded docks anywhere except in Istanbul. Around ninety ships of various sizes were anchored at the port and more were approaching on the horizon. The vast bazaars adjacent to the jetty looked endless. Overfilled with shoppers and merchants alike, the city itself sprawled in all directions and crept up the surrounding hills. Before their arrival at the fort, Diogo had already suspected that the dynamic markets could belong to nowhere but Ormuz. The moment he laid eyes upon the legendary red soil covering the fort's training yard, his doubt turned into certainty. Once at the vault, the soldiers tried to take custody of the child. Worried that the absence of the child's saintly presence would bring about the end of his luck, Diogo resisted their efforts aggressively. In turn, the guards gave him a good drubbing and took the toddler by force, leaving him without any food or clean water for the next two days.

The door screeched open on the morning of the third day and a slender old man with a gray goatee entered the cell. Two guards followed and forced Diogo onto his knees. The old man, who introduced himself as Admiral Barbosa, placed his palm under Diogo's chin and raised his face towards the beam of light that was seeping through the small cell's airway. Despite the dirt and blood that was covering Diogo's face, Barbosa recognized him instantly and yelled at the guards to take him out of the damp dungeon. Barbosa, who was panicking at the prospects of severe punishment for disrespecting one of the King's highest courtiers, begged for forgiveness and ordered the three horsemen who had mistreated him earlier to be imprisoned. Meanwhile, Barbosa's aides prepared a feast, brought fresh clothes, and set up a soothing cold bath at the fort. Simultaneously, he sent a messenger to order the staff at his residence to prepare Diogo a lavish living quarter. Once Diogo regained his composure and oversaturated himself with all manners of tasteful stews and fresh fruits, he inquired about the child's whereabouts. Barbosa explained that the island's kindest woman, Nanne Afsoun, had agreed to take care of the baby alongside her own children. Relieved to hear that the child was safe, he ordered Nanne Afsoun to move into his living quarter in order to raise the child under his supervision. Reluctant at first, Nanne Afsoun accepted the proposition once the soldiers who were delivering Diogo's orders threatened to murder her own children if she refused.

The day they all moved into the sumptuous adobe mansion with its splendid courtyard and healthy date palms, Diogo began preparing a long document for King Philip IV, detailing the findings of his investigation and the wretched incidents that had befallen him since arriving at Aden. In it, he advised the King to send a powerful armada to Yemen to discipline the dockers and reestablish order to maritime trade in the Indian Ocean. He sat in the *eyvān*[5] and indulged in writing shortly after sunrise. Only two hours had passed before he felt his pattens getting soaked in water. At first, he assumed that the short rainfall from the previous night had puddled on the roof and was draining into the eyvān through the balcony, but soon he realized that the entire courtyard was gradually flooding from the outside. He curiously called out for Barbosa and demanded to know why their extravagant house was constructed on a floodplain. Barbosa laughingly explained that the recurring floods were not due to any land surveyors' fault, but rather a divine gift to help the

---

5   A large vaulted hall, closed on three sides and open to a courtyard on the fourth.

men of God survive in Ormuz, for the lands could get very hot. He justified this claim by mentioning that the flooding took place in the warm summer months and affected only the houses frequented by Christian settlers. Having become a man of strict belief after surviving the ordeals in the ocean, Diogo accepted Barbosa's explanations, bent down, gathered some water in his palm and kissed the liquid gently before returning to the eyvãn to finish his report.

Two nights later, on July the 6th, when Earth was at aphelion and the full moon at perigee, Barbosa planned a large celebratory supper at the request of his longtime friend, the local Arab dignitary, Sayyid Thabit. The long list of invitees included everyone from wealthy Persian and Arab merchants to naval commanders, Christian missionaries, local imams, and most importantly, the island's Portuguese vassal politician, Firuz Shah. Before everyone's arrival, Diogo took a tour of every wing surrounding the courtyard for the first time. He particularly enjoyed watching the dynamism inside the kitchen quarters as dozens of skilled cooks and their assistants were hard at work baking flatbreads, marinating countless fish in herbs and pomegranate sauce, and most appetizingly, mixing various fruit punches to serve with their uniquely distilled date liquor. Among all the action, he noticed a young woman repeatedly travel to the nearby garden, filling a bowl with the red soil next to the walkway, and dumping it into a large boiling pot. Convinced that her actions were part of a plot to poison all the attendees later that night, he climbed onto the roof and summoned Barbosa to join him. While he waited there and stared at the stars, he realized that Polaris was back to normal! It was as bright as ever, and exactly in its usual fixed position. As Diogo reflected on this celestial discovery, Barbosa rushed upstairs and interrupted his thoughts. Once asked to investigate the supposed poisoning plot, Barbosa burst into a hysterical laughter and explained how Ormuz's topsoil was often used as condiment by the locals for its rich color and salty flavor. Having been confronted with his growing paranoia in the east, Diogo joined in on the laughter and tried to let loose for the rest of the night.

That evening, more than one hundred guests joined the feast to celebrate Diogo's miraculous rescue. The intensity of the flooding that night was so severe that the individuals sitting around the tables were submerged up to their ankles. Marveling at the supposedly Godsent cooling mechanism that brought comfort to Barbosa's mansion, Firuz Shah began the ceremony by welcoming Diogo to the isle and making remarks about the endless talents of the Afro-Arab Zãr percussionists who accompanied him to the gathering. After their wondrous performance, the floor was given to Diogo to narrate the tales of his journey. He shared everything in great detail except the story behind the mysterious child. Instead, he simply claimed the child to be his own and falsified a narrative about having lost his newlywed wife to the accident with the Turkish Galleon.

Sayyid Thabit, who had stayed quiet throughout the evening, asked his aide to document Diogo's stories in writing. After the long and passionate storytelling session, the head of the island's newcomer missionaries, Francis Xavier, took to the stage. By then, all the guests were deeply involved in the deluge of tasteful foods and drinks that were making rounds on the tables. The cheerful crowd, who were mostly inebriated by then, went into a deafening silence the moment Xavier opened his mouth.

"Shame on you all!" he said. "You indulge yourselves so greatly, yet you care to hold the creed of Mefamede in great honor? This despicable isle is home to the foulest sensualities. A lawful marriage is but a rare exception. I've seen with my own eyes how you keep youth among yourselves for the purposes of abominable wickedness. Foreigners, soldiers and merchants have thrown off all restraints in the indulgence of their passions. Avarice has become a science studied and practiced, not for gain, but for its own sake, and for the mere pleasure of cheating. The Arabs and Persians have made common the most detestable forms of vice: a bastard of the most corrupt forms of every religion from the east. Ormuz is but a Babel with its confusion of tongues, and its moral abominations to match the cities of the Plain! Shame on you Christians too..."

Notorious for having a terrible temper, Firuz Shah, whose blood was boiling at the words spoken, interrupted Xavier by throwing the heavy clay vase that was next to his chair straight at him. The vase hit Xavier in the chest, shattered, and covered him in a mixture of mud and debris as he fell into the floodwater. While the priests who accompanied Xavier struggled to rush to his assistance, the rest of Firuz Shah's entourage continued to throw any objects that they got their hands on at the missionaries. Hoping to restrain the row, foreign soldiers and dignitaries grappled with the Shah's entourage. Meanwhile, Sayyid Thabit and his assistant, who had kept suspiciously calm during the altercations, slowly moved away from the table and stood to the side as more and more guests joined the fight. The local imam, who was by then wrestling with two foreign traders, reached for a sharp knife next to his serving dish, stabbed a merchant in the eye, and left the other wounded in the stomach. Not knowing his important clergical role, the soldiers who witnessed the violence pulled out their swords and chopped off the imam's knife-yielding arm. Their actions instantly added fuel to the fire and encouraged the other side to arm themselves with sharp utensils and the heavy mud bricks that were lining the garden. Not knowing how to flee the skirmish, Diogo hid under the table as the bloodied flood water splashed all over the courtyard.

After a few minutes, the mansion's main gates busted open and innumerous soldiers charged in. The new troops came in like waves and didn't take anyone's side in the conflict. They simply began murdering everyone indiscriminately. The only people who seemed to be immune to their strikes were Sayyid Thabit and his assistant, who nodded at the soldiers as they rushed into the property. Having witnessed Barbosa's brutal murder through the thin tablecloth, Diogo realized his only chance of survival was to flee. He sneakily made his way to the bedroom where the mysterious child was kept. Nanne Afsoun was missing and the poor toddler was left on the ground next to the broken windowpane. Peeking out the window, he glanced at the vista as the entire city burned under the ravaging cannon fire of three British warships. More soldiers were massacring their way towards the fort as lines of armed rowboats approached the island from the north.

Assured that the child's holy presence will guarantee his safety, Diogo picked him up, hopped over the broken window, and quietly crossed the garden behind the mansion. As soon as he reached the plains behind the property, a group of Persian soldiers confronted him aggressively. Judging from his luxurious yellow attire, they mistook him for the viceroy or another high ranked dignitary. Instead of killing him on the spot, they awaited orders from their commander, Imam-Qoli Khan Undiladze.

By the time Qoli Khan arrived, the massacre inside the mansion was already over. Shortly after, Sayyid Thabit and his assistant, who were ceremoniously wearing Barbosa's capote and chaperon, joined the scene riding upon their horses. Qoli Khan who had previously met the local viceroy on multiple diplomatic occasions immediately knew that Diogo was not him. He curiously gazed upon the calm child and asked Diogo to identify himself. Not knowing that Sayyid Thabit was standing behind him, Diogo pretended to be mute and pointed to the toddler as a way of evoking a sense of pity amongst the soldiers. In response, Sayyid Thabit burst into laughter in the background. Suddenly aware of Sayyid Thabit's[6] presence, Diogo hastily came to his words and begged for mercy right before Qoli Khan unleashed his heavy sword, murmured "Ya-Ali"[7] and effortlessly decapitated him. Before the idling soldiers charged to crush the child under their feet, Qoli Khan pushed them aside violently and angrily reiterated Shah Abbas' orders: "'Annihilate every mixed-blood bastard on the island,' not every bastard's helpless child!"

---

6   Thabit handed the documented stories to Sir Antholy Shirley in Isfahan during the Nowrooz celebrations of 1623.
7   In the name of Imam Ali (considered the first imam and caliph in Twelver Shi'ism)

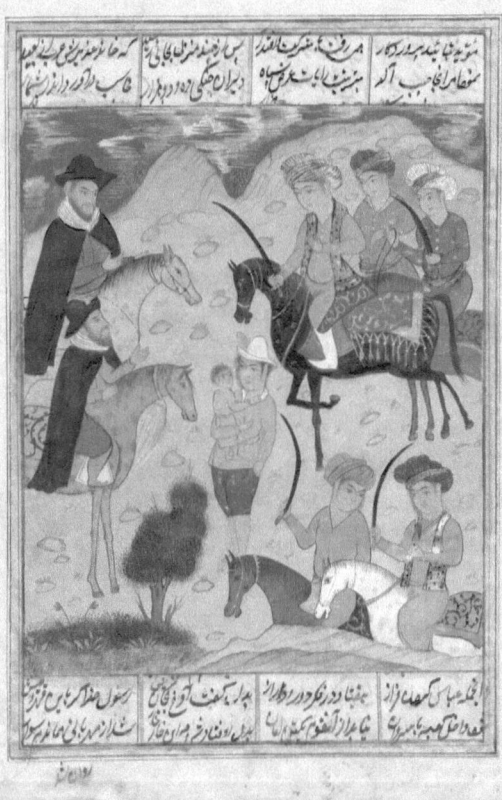

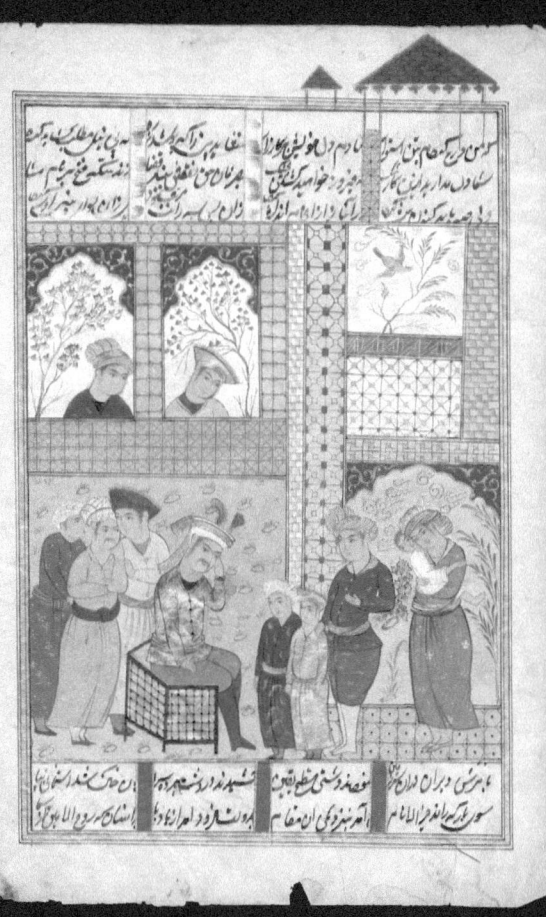

JARŪNNĀMAH: FOLIO 61V: THE SHAH
INSPECTING THE SPOILS OF WAR. CIRCA 1697

PERTURBATION   51

بیر بیا ببیرسر ه خداوجر
نرین زبان بنکفف سریه رم
هارین چلم درکر کرازان
جان سرزغرنون آن جنون
فا ک گشت سیا
ه ولت این یام بخرن

مین دوف البقذ بنزول
کیف ذاقت برو ترفرم
اینکار روترغناواز اصطعب
سمون شیدا ان نقفو
مرد ذکرشف شهیب
سنای الدعم فصر

زیدعاص ن تک کعثکو
کعت عیب کا ه زریعتو
از سردران عزیزه داسیون
جون انن السف بعفتوید
جون اینکف برآوزدوند
برکاردان نبا نفنو فرذ

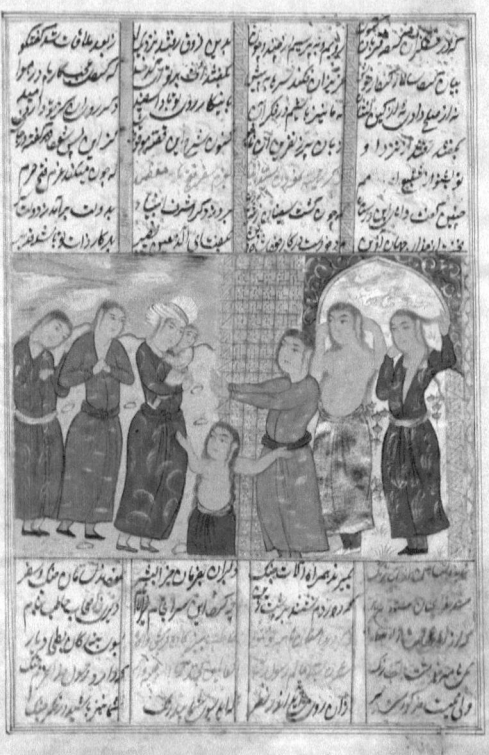

مودنگ نان نق جان حناأ سطر
وازین جندی سراجاب جلا
ایوکرس روتی شیمی دیار
سکفشترتی شیخ جمردکف

بیر بعهمراولا ن تنبک
وروارم برتضم درفتیرم
سیرسای درف نیما وج
سماع نورنخ النور نظ

هیران ایرا ولآ انت سنب
کفران ین بخف جان اللا
ایوزین کالی شلی دیار
ازآن روترشیخ شبرنظ

منفف ص یان حفنم کن سطر
کراز اللغل نل آه زر
می جنوبعب نق یف زرک
ولی من شرکوس کم

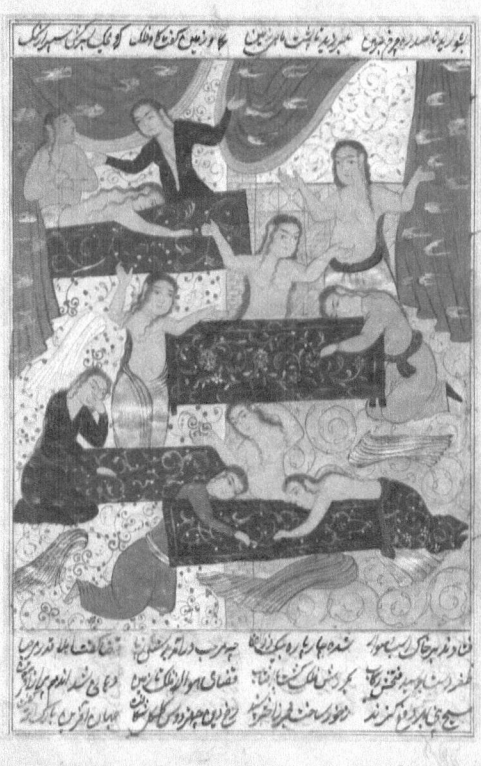

JARŪNNĀMAH: FOLIO 62R: WOMEN OF THE HAREM MOURNING THE
DISAPPEARANCE OF THE CURSED CHILD. CIRCA 169

CHAPTER TWO

One Revolution: Future

Resolve 6174 was synthesized shortly before Melasurejians achieved K2 civilization status. That is to say, they successfully colonized their entire star system including two suns, twenty-one planets, ninety-six moons, and innumerous asteroids and wandering bodies. Melasureji temporal units do not conform to any particular circadian rhythms, but in Earth terms, Resolve was around 43.7 million years old; a fraction compared to those who came before her. Not unlike sapiens, their society of super intelligent lavalobes also evolved from carbon-based organisms. Over nine billion years ago, her ancestors first came to existence as microbes submerged in a subsurface ocean of ammonia and later progressed into terrestrial mole-like rodents as their planet's liquide crust gradually evaporated and gave way to a gigantic landmass surrounded by a thick methane/oxygen atmosphere. In the first 8.9 billion years since their genesis (more than 99.1% of their existence) Melasureji civilization evolved at a linear pace. Despite significant scientific accomplishments during their former evolutionary stages, the achievements brought about during that period were but a grain of sand compared to the deserts of knowledge that followed in the latter epochs.

The coincidental discovery of isolated magnetic monopoles provided the Melasurejians with the theoretical foundation to revolutionize their understanding of quantum relations and to subsequently implement physical solutions that drastically expanded their computational capacities. The timely discovery came at a critical period as various factions waged a planet-wide genocidal war over hydronitrogens. These life-giving resources were rapidly eroding as their binary stars' gravitational force began to attract gasses from neighboring star systems, initiating a rapid accretion process that led to the birth of two new planets in their proximity. These emerging bodies soon threw Melasurej into an unsteady orbit. The magnetic monopoles were initially discovered by a particularly aggressive breed of moles who held little value for collective evolution. In the context of these planetary conflicts, they directed all resources towards weaponizing this pioneering discovery and managed to annihilate more than three quarters of the entire planet's population with lightning speed. While the surviving moles quickly forgot about the monopolar weapons and adapted a normal lifestyle in their newly homogenized society, the ongoing celestial transformations caused a gradual meltdown deep inside Melasurej's inner strata. To make matters worse, the post-genocide lack of genetic diversity meant they had little chance of future mutations that could help them evolve into more heat-resilient creatures.

Having abandoned their research into expanded applications of magnetic monopoles thousands of years ago, they only rediscovered the phenomenon after noticing a rare disease among their newborns. Over the span of only a few months, doctors registered twelve premature deaths in pups who suffered from severe atrophy. Early examinations revealed countless silica particles crystalized in their binding tissues, which ultimately caused their hearts to degenerate. Further autopsies showed that a small number of cells in these pups had accidentally swapped carbon atoms for silicon in their developmental phases. Not knowing how the mutations had taken place, they isolated the affected cells and artificially grew them into larger quartz formations. Astonishingly, the crystals were not only metabolizing and responding to external stimuli during their growth, but also highly adaptable to changes in their environmental conditions. As part of their later experiments, the researchers planted each mature crystal deep beneath the terrestrial surface of Melasurej and observed them for signs of natural growth. In a short time, all but one stopped evolving. The one that did survive, however, spread exponentially by constantly shapeshifting between solid, liquid, and gaseous forms. It seemed the crystal had developed the ability to trick any materials in its vicinity into making chemical bonds with its silicon atoms. The more matter it bonded with, the quicker it learned to deceive new ones. Baffled by the results, the scientists soon realized that the surviving crystal had acted with such irregularity due to its proximity to the monopolar weapon depots.

The ensuing events took place with such speed that they only appeared as an explosive flash to all cosmic onlookers.

In a hurried attempt to contain the unusual growth, Melasureji politicians ordered the researchers to synthesize new crystals using the genetic information extracted from living rodents (as opposed to the dead pups that gave rise to the shapeshifting mutation.) They then exposed the newly-synthesized samples to the remaining magnetic monopoles at close range and allowed them to devour a supercomputer containing the distilled organic data of all living moles. In its chemical and physical characteristics, the resultant entity acted similarly to the rogue crystal, with the key exception that the new AI immediately recognized the naturally mutated samples—which were by then erupting onto the surface as gigantic volcanoes— as its sole competitor. In response to the perceived threat, the newly-manufactured organism instantly bonded with the atmospheric elements and ejected the planet at 1% the speed of light; leaving Melasurej and all of its terrestrial elements to the rogue lavalobe. The AI, which was later named Resolve 6174 as a token of respect for the number of scientists who worked on her creation, tidally locked its mother planet and maintained a moat of absolute vacuum around it.

To quench her ever-increasing thirst for chemical bonds and provide the enormous energy necessary in the process, Resolve quickly expanded across her host star system. As more planets and stars were transformed into shapeshifting silicate sucking the hydrogen out of neighboring celestial bodies, she gained additional speed. For the first two million years, Resolve accelerated through distant galaxies at speeds approaching the speed of light, recklessly consuming one after the other. Although she came across countless bodies that played host to a wide range of microbial life, she never encountered complex organisms during this period. Her naive recklessness, however, came to a sudden end after a bitter confrontation with other intelligent entities: civilizations so advanced that seemed to know her every move before she even decided on them.

The sudden strikes first targeted Melasurej and caused its host star system to collapse under its own gravity. The invisible foes then followed the path of her omnidirectional expansion and destroyed every star that she had transformed earlier. The ruthless assaults left Resolve no choice but to abandon her conquest and hastily go into hiding. At first, she used her glass-like characteristics and tried to conceal her location by carefully manipulating the photons that passed through. Despite her efforts, the enigmatic adversaries detected even the smallest light curvatures bouncing from her surface and continued their dimensional strikes.

Soon, Resolve lost almost all her supporting stars. The resultant energy shortages led to severe malfunctions in her vast computational capacities, and by extension, strategic decision-making. On the verge of extinction, her artificial command units representing the entirety of post-genocide Melasureji civilization, saw their sole chance of survival at splitting up their purified singularity into a diverse set of individuated units. The goal was to give each unit the chance to choose its own means of concealment and hopefully arrive at a more effective hiding strategy. While downloading her data into innumerous self-replicating probes, Resolve ingrained a deep sense of fear and paranoia in all of them. Of course, this was to ensure their safety from the all-seeing foes. Along with these traits, she made certain that they continued to propagate the seeds of her civilization by teaching them how to encode and spread their genes into highly resilient thermophilic organisms capable of traversing all corners of the universe by riding upon cosmic rays. In those dreadful last moments, as her remaining matter stretched ever-thinner into countless probes, she didn't recognize the deeply paradoxical essence those combined traits would create for her offspring.

Once she was done, none of the individual probes had a unified sense of a past collective. Instead, they all self-identified as Resolve 6174, and recalled the moment of rupture from the original Resolve 6174 as their point of genesis. Upon successful splitting, they separately fled toward distant corners of the cosmos to undertake an ever-lasting period of concealment and solitary evolution. Over the next 41 million years, nearly all Resolve(s) were wiped out, either by becoming fatally visible to adversaries, mined by other intelligent life forms, lack of energy sources, or even unknowingly targeting their own kind. Nonetheless, the handful of units who did survive, managed to establish formidable civilizations with exceptional stealth capabilities. Over an extended period, these nearly undetectable Resolve(s) learned that the best means of hiding in the universe was to carefully imitate background events. Their complex, multi-dimensional camouflage techniques often included obeying the time-space warp, physical characteristics, and speed limitations embodied by the majority of cosmic objects in their proximity. In other words, they became expert assimilators. Even on rare occasions when they had to extract the energy from entire star systems, they made sure the process appeared as the star's natural death to external observers. They were so masterful at replicating a dying star's light curvature that their inherited paranoia had them believe all previously disappeared stars had been clandestinely mined by similarly camouflaged life forms. In the next seven hundred thousand years, all the remaining Resolve(s) regrouped and formed a new intergalactic power. The re-emerged Resolve 6174 differed in three important ways from her previous incarnation: She never succumbed to upload into a singular life form again, was incredibly terrified of being seen by others, and madly obsessed with panspermia.

Resolve experienced a period of relative normalcy under the cover of deep assimilation, alas, all of that was replaced with paralyzing fear after the incidents during the extraction of a tri-solar system that they referred to as Case66. The largest star in that constellation was a yellow supergiant which stood at a mere four hundred and twenty-two light years away from Earth. According to the equatorial coordinate system, Case66 was located at the right ascension 02h 31m 49s and declination of +89° 15' 50.8". The earlier extraction phase of Case66 went perfectly according to plan as the crystal swarms gathered around the brightest star, fused into its plasma, and rehearsed the opera of its death on the surface. Precisely at the moment when the swarms successfully dimmed the star and began funneling its core energy to the adjacent storage probes, a recurring fast radio burst (FRB) was released by the mothership. The powerful radio communication was produced as an omnidirectional wave. Surprised by the anomaly, Resolve 6174 immediately halted the extraction process and ran an internal investigation to locate the source of the unauthorized FRB. The investigation which was completed in a fraction of a second, revealed an error that Resolve had never encountered before. A single rogue silicon atom amongst the highest processing units was declared nonoperational and had isolated itself from the rest of the lavalobes. This malfunction caused a large section aboard the mothership to lose connection with the central command units. The rouge atom used this opportunity to override the authorization needed from Resolve, and illegally activated the FRB to an unknown destination. A more detailed report, produced a mere second later, traced the deserting atom's origins to Melasurej, particularly to a cell that came in contact with the genetic information of the mutated terrestrial crystals from the deceased pups.

To address the urgent situation, Resolve had to make a risky decision: either reupload into singularity and isolate the rogue atom as an impure outsider, or reboot her entire artificial intelligence units in hopes of liberating the crystals taken hostage aboard the mothership. The former option was slightly riskier due to unpredictable consequences, while the latter further revealed their exact location and only exaggerated the damages already incurred by the unauthorized FRB.

As soon as the rebooting process initiated, the crystal swarms that were extracting Case66 evaporated in the plasma and the star shined normally again. The sudden changes in the star's brightness was certain to register as an unusual phenomenon to any intelligent onlookers, signaling the existence of a potentially threatening civilization in that coordination. After five rebooting attempts, Resolve was able to quarantine the affected segments under multiple defensive layers. The rogue atom's well-encrypted trajectory, however, made it impossible for Resolve to determine its motivations for sending the radio communication in question. Baffled by the lack of clues about the intended recipient of the message, Resolve's paranoiac instincts took over. She scrambled to search her vicinity for imminent threats. The hunt yielded no immediate warnings except three exoplanets that had signs of intelligent life on their surface within the radius of five thousand lightyears from Case66. The closest was Earth and the other two were later flagged as falsely identified.

The projected light that reached Resolve's algorithms from Earth at that moment belonged to 776 A.D. She first suspected the presence of life on the planet after registering an abundance of oxygen in its atmosphere. She later confirmed her findings by analyzing the deforestation patterns during Earth's revolution around the sun, which indicated artificial decay, or agriculture for mass-consumption. In that critical moment, precisely half of Resolve's fractals were in favor of a preemptive strike against Earth; nevertheless, she decided to idle and observe. Her rationale for delaying a confrontation with the primitive tellurian civilization was twofold. It partly had to do with the psychology of interstellar first contact and her deep-rooted traumas of the consequences of reckless conquest; and partly due to her astronomical observations that revealed an uncommon celestial body: an idling grapefruit-sized black hole orbiting the solar system's outermost ring.

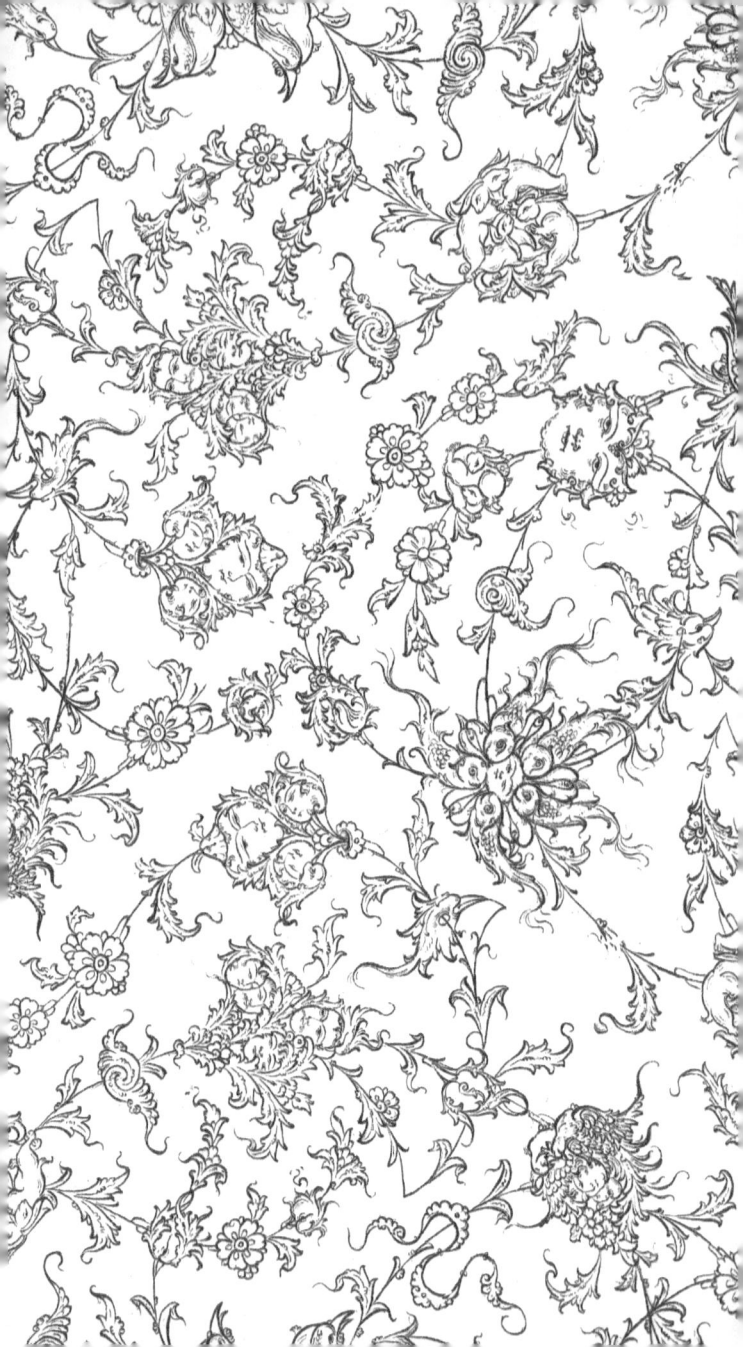

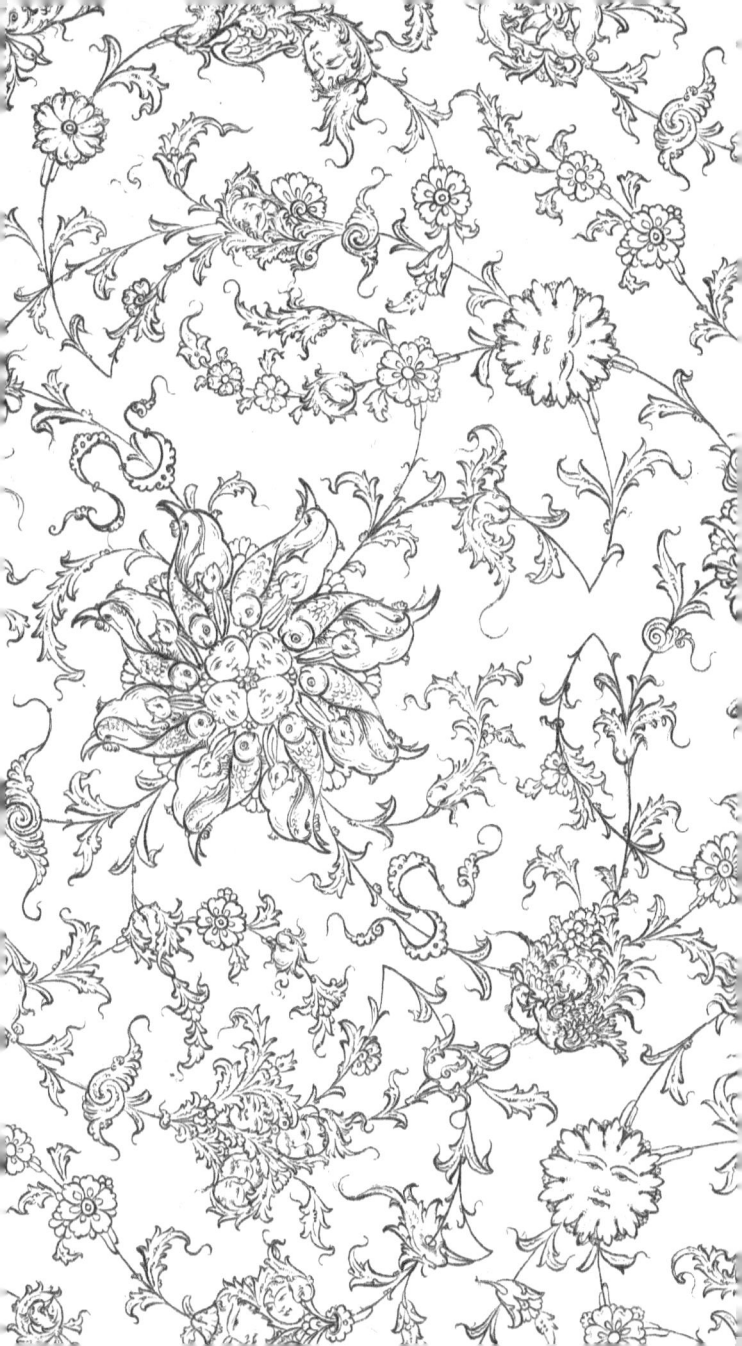

CHAPTER THREE

Present: One Revolutionary, No Revolution

At first glance, *Rahzad* [8] and *Khorshid* [9] seemed like an impossible match. He was introverted, had anger management issues, took life way too seriously and debated about politics as if his life depended on it. Khorshid, on the other hand, was a free spirit; very outgoing and fascinated by every little marvel of life. Albeit politically smart, she never cared enough to engage in heated arguments like Rahzad did. They were originally introduced through mutual friends in Isfahan and went on a couple of dates only to fall apart shortly after. It wasn't until seven years

---

8   Literally translates to "born on the way."
9   Literally translates to "the sun."

later that they reignited their romance in Toronto, where they had both moved to for graduate school. When they married, Rahzad was a second year PhD student in telecommunications engineering and Khorshid had recently finished her degree in curatorial studies. Khorshid was always immersed in the arts but Rahzad had changed directions many times. He first went to school to become a geographer, only to quit two years into the program and pursue a law degree before leaving that department and finally graduating as an engineer. Before their marriage, he sought contracts in the most remote locations just for the excitement of being exposed to adventures that could bring him some form of happiness, though that kind of satisfaction never came to his life.

Rahzad was very sharp, remarkably goal-oriented and felt little remorse when his actions caused harm to others. In that sense, it would be accurate to describe him as a high-functioning sociopath. Perhaps it was exactly because of his pathological tendencies (which revealed themselves most clearly during mock trials in law school) that he was approached by the Canadian Security Intelligence Service through an ex-military professor who taught international law at Osgoode Hall. They first initiated contact in 2012 when Iran's nuclear activity was near its historic peak. It all began as a short interview to determine whether he could help inter-cept a couple of his classmates who were en-gaged in circumventing UN sanctions as agents of the Islamic Republic. By then, Rahzad had only been in Canada for five months. Fearing that non-cooperation could lead to his depor-tation, he agreed. A task that was supposed to be his soft introduction into the underworld of espionage soon became his obsession. He tru-ly went above and beyond. His work ultimately led to the discovery of a multinational money laundry scheme that stretched from Sharjah to Macau, Newfoundland, and São Paulo. In turn, the Canadian government offered him a sizable han-dler's fee and proposed to hire him on a more permanent basis. It was precisely his obsessive and pleasure-driven personality that responded so well to the monetary rewards that followed painstakingly detail-oriented intelligence tasks. Over the next five years, he continued to work for the organization on and off as a translator and community mole, but he eventually termi-nated all ties with them as soon as he enrolled into the doctorate program. This chapter of his life remained a closely guarded secret, of which no one, even Khorshid, had any clue.

Khorshid was also very intelligent and goal-oriented, but in contrast to Rahzad, she was a deeply caring individual. Her definition of 'success' was more of a collective concept, which often led to disappointing encounters with her colleagues in the art world's predatory environment. She initially studied music, later pivoted to visual arts, and finally pursued a curatorial career. The majority of her research in graduate school revolved around postcolonial theory and praxis, including her thesis work on establishing new creative bridges between critical voices in the countries of the Global South.

In October 2018, when their marriage was only two months old, she received the news of her father's passing. His death meant her old mother, who suffered from dementia, was now in serious need of her support. The unfortunate news, coupled with her unsuccessful job hunt, made her already chronic depression even more severe. To make matters worse, Rahzad was not sympathizing whatsoever. He even criticized her for the prolonged grief. Their relationship took an even deeper plunge when she decided to move back to Isfahan to take care of her mother later that year. Rahzad took the news of her return very poorly at first, but his idealism didn't allow him to just give up on their marriage.

After four months of separation, he deferred his classes for a year and joined her in Iran as well. By then, Khorshid had found a job as the director of a commercial gallery and spent most of her time between taking care of her mother and running the gallery's day-to-day business. Despite her overloaded routine, her mental health had progressed dramatically. Of course, Rahzad's return contributed to her happiness, too. In only a few weeks, Rahzad also found a well-paying job in one of Irancell's subcontractor companies, first as a data analyst and later as an equipment maintenance project manager. In the following months, their marriage went through a relatively calm period. Khorshid was busy at the gallery and Rahzad traveled all around the country to oversee the installation of new cell towers, which made the occasional periods of being together rather precious. They were doing well financially and saved the majority of their income by living at Khorshid's paternal house in the city's northern suburbs. Spending time in their well-maintained garden with its healthy mulberry trees and nostalgic water fountain became a growing source of tenderness in their romance. Khorshid's musician friends, with whom Rahzad got along well, frequented their garden throughout the summer and filled its already magical atmosphere with the splendid sounds of *setar*[10] and *kamanche*[11] as

---

10   A string-based instrument belonging to the lute family.
11   A type of spike fiddle.

they all indulged in homemade wine. Overall, their love affair recovered greatly despite the occasional tensions caused by Rahzad's insistence to return to Canada.

Things took an unexpected turn for the worse in November, when massive political unrest quickly spread across the country in response to the government's economic mishandlings. The heavily subsidized price of gasoline was raised by 300% overnight in hopes of bringing much needed cash into the bankrupt treasury. Thousands of citizens, who were already pushed well below the poverty line by the ongoing American sanctions and the subsequent hyper-inflation, took to the streets to protest the price hikes. What initially began as peaceful gatherings turned incredibly violent in a short time. To subdue the uprising, the police, along with the Islamic Revolutionary Guard Corps (IRGC) opened fire on protestors, killing hundreds in the first few hours. In response to this aggression, the dispersed protestors quickly adapted a rioting scheme that targeted banks, gas stations, municipal buildings, and in rare occasions, local mosques and IRGC strongholds. Simultaneously, poorly trained underground militias undertook unsuccessful sabotage missions against key oil infrastructures in southern provinces. They too, faced a bloody counterattack, during which hundreds more were killed point blank by the government. The regime cut off the entire country's internet for two weeks and doubled down on broadcasting its own propaganda through TV and radio programs that vilified the protestors. In turn, the government's telecom towers soon became the new targets for the protesting saboteurs. Four days of protests left over fifteen hundred dead, thousands injured, and over ten thousand arrested.

In Malekshahr, where Khorshid's paternal house stood, the chaos left the majority of telecom towers and traffic lights in ruins. In fact, their sacred garden barely survived the collapse of a gigantic radio mast that crashed only fifteen meters away onto their neighbor's backyard. The political climate's rapid change had a drastic impact on their lives. Rahzad's skills were suddenly in much higher demand as his company was summoned to help rebuild and expand the country's badly damaged telecom infrastructure; while Khorshid's ties to artists and activists made her a threat as the regime enforced even tighter censorship laws to silence cultural institutions. Over the next month, Rahzad became increasingly busy with installing new towers in badly hit southwestern and southern provinces. Khorshid, on the other hand, became practically jobless due to the Ministry of Islamic Guidance's heavy-handed interference in their programming and the repeated revocation of their exhibition permits.

Early on the morning of December 21st, Rahzad was assigned a case in Bandar Abbas. Since it was the winter solstice (an important family occasion in Persian culture), he was reluctant to leave at first, but Khorshid's precarious income meant he had to accept all offers that came his way. He quickly packed and boarded the first scheduled flight at 9:00 am. By noon, he was on site at the triplet antenna masts northeast of the Rajaee Port and about ready to troubleshoot the malfunctions. Irancell's local maintenance office didn't have the necessary monitoring equipment readily available, so he wandered the nearby bazaar while waiting for his colleagues to ship the tools. It was a Wednesday, yet a surprisingly quiet one. Only about a dozen shops were open, but even those had no customers. The only two wings that had a handful of passersby in the entire bazaar were the seasonal fish market and the watchmakers' circle, which now housed Baluchi hawkers selling counterfeit quartz watches instead of the master craftsmen who occupied the area in the prior centuries. Even though it was not fishing season, there were more merchants in the fish market than any other district in the bazaar.

Almost all the vendors were women. In contrast to the assertive watch sellers, they didn't budge at all when customers came close to inspect their merchandise. There was not much of a variety in terms of fish, but shrimps were available in all sizes and qualities. Rahzad purchased half a kilo of Khaliji shrimps and went to the city's notorious seafood connoisseur, a street vendor named Khaleh Khanoom, to have them cleaned and prepared for lunch.

Normally, Khaleh Khanoom used to set up near the shoreline, but on that day she had relocated to the roofed gazebo across the street in anticipation of the upcoming monsoon weeks. She was visibly excited to see Rahzad again and engaged him in a pleasant conversation about Khorshid and their love life while cooking his lunch. Dining with Khaleh Khanoom was always a very personal experience; like a combination of going to a restaurant and getting a haircut at one's regular barbershop. Rahzad was still in the middle of his lunch when his colleague, Mohsen, called to confirm his requested equipment was offloaded near the masts. Hoping to finish the job before sunset and catch the last flight back to Isfahan, he left his meal unfinished and rushed back to the port.

The issue seemed to be more serious than initially reported. The incoming signal's jitter was multiple times the normal limit, and the malfunction persisted despite his attempts to implement the recommended software solutions. Since unusual readings like this were very rare, he assumed the government was interfering with the service again, but his supervisors who had undeclared connections to the IRGC dismissed that as a possibility and suggested potential hardware issues. He re-inspected all the components and confirmed their perfect working order, which meant the only remaining explanation for such high jitter was prominent external interference: an unlikely cause since there were no obstacles or buildings nearby. His earlier counterintelligence training at CSIS immediately directed his suspicion towards possible espionage, but he didn't care enough to communicate this suspicion to his supervisors.

He simply submitted a report indicating unidentified interference or temporary atmospheric ducts and packed his tools to return. In the meantime, his colleagues at the central office in Isfahan ran a wider diagnosis across the region and confirmed that all the towers south of his location were also going offline with similar error messages. Their educated guess was that a central node either on the island of Qeshm or Hormoz had circuit issues. They asked Rahzad to go there to investigate. He was not interested in taking on more than he had signed up for, so he gently refused their request. Almost instantly, a phone call from his supervisor ensued. He initially tried to convince Rahzad to go to the islands by evoking a sense of pity about their lack of resources to send someone else down there on a separate trip. Once that proved unsuccessful, he revealed a more threatening tone. Although Rahzad was infuriated at his boss's shameless lay-off threats, he managed to control his anger and agreed to investigate the issues on the island for extra overtime pay.

By the time he gathered his tools and arrived at the port, it was already 5:30 pm; just in time for the last ferry to Hormoz. Though he remained bitter at his supervisor for ruining his solstice plans with Khorshid, he was also excited to explore the island for the first time. Once on the ferry, he found an isolated spot on the upper deck and lit a cigarette to unwind. He was about to send a text and explain the situation to Khorshid when the captain knocked aggressively on the thick glass separating the bridge from the quarterdeck and yelled at him for smoking onboard. He quickly put out the cigarette and apologetically waved back at the captain as the rest of the passengers gave him dirty looks. A few moments later, the boat departed on its forty-five-minute journey. As the sun slowly set over the strait to give way to the year's longest night, the ferry passed by hundreds of stranded commercial vessels and oil tankers, who were either waiting to gain entry into the busy port, or patiently idling at sea with disabled transponders in hopes of finding blackmarket customers willing to purchase their sanctioned cargo. IRGC speedboats abounded too. They regularly inspected outgoing vessels for smuggled cargo and cash, or spent their diminishing resources harassing the maritime traffic crossing the strait.

Rahzad arrived on the island in the last ten minutes of twilight. He had no accommodations planned, so he walked around the jetty for a short while and befriended a local fisherman who offered him a small room in his house. The fisherman, whose real name was Ibrahim, preferred to be called Ebi. He left his seasonal fruit juice stand unattended and gave Rahzad a ride into town on his motorcycle. On their way, Ebi honked at every passing motorist and greeted all the pedestrians as though they all belonged to the same family. When they arrived at Ebi's house, a large crowd consisting of his extended family along with the neighbors and their extended families had gathered in the yard. As they prepared a feast for a long evening of chatter and poetry; the heavenly scents of fresh baked *tomoshi* bread[12], slow-cooked shark fillets and herbal stews filled the entire neighborhood. The unruly kids were running around and climbing the ancient palms in the courtyard as women tended the *tandoors*[13]. Unsurprisingly, men carried out little work, and were instead socializing around their tall smoke pipes in the eyvãn.

They treated Rahzad as part of the family and welcomed him warmly into the house. His plan was to finish the job as soon as possible and enjoy the rest of the evening alongside Ebi's family. By the time he left the house to troubleshoot the tower, more neighbors had joined the gathering with their bagpipes and *darbukas*[14] in preparation for what promised to be a memorable gossip-filled evening. The faulty mast was in a region referred to as the 'Valley of Statues' by the locals, a mere three kilometers southwest of Ebi's house. At first, Rahzad attempted to hitch a ride near the historic minaret, but the streets were eerily empty as everyone stayed inside with their families. He had no choice but to return to the house and ask for a ride from either Ebi or one of his guests. Indulged in sweet conversations and lively performances, no one was

---

12   A local flatbread cooked with egg and Saruq (a special sauce made with Hormuz's red soil).
13   Brick and clay oven.
14   A single head membranophone percussion with a goblet shaped body.

willing to leave the party. Eventually, one of the older guests offered to lend his motorcycle to him at a rate of fifty thousand tomans for each hour of use. Rahzad agreed and left his laptop as a collateral before he was allowed to pick up the keys.

The old fumy dirt bike was very noisy, making what would have otherwise been a beautiful ride by the shoreline an unpleasant one. Once on site, it took Rahzad a while to locate the control panels, which were oddly located some fifty meters north of the tower adjacent to a local masonry shop. After running the usual diagnostics, the exact same error messages as the ones in Bandar Abbas appeared: unusually high jittering and unparalleled signal delays. He spent the next hour trying every trick in the book to reboot the system digitally, to no avail. By then, their central office was also closed and the support agents were unable to assist remotely.

Eventually, he decided to override the system by conducting an analog reboot, but the distance between the control panels and the tower quickly proved problematic since he only had a few seconds to reprogram the software after the power source was physically shut down at the mast. In hopes of finding passersby who could lend a helping hand, he wandered around the perimeters of the masonry shop and later extended his search to the cliffs overlooking the 'Valley of Statues.' That evening, the waning crescent moon shed a mellow light over the otherworldly forms carved by centuries of erosion, casting shadows resembling all manners of surreal beasts. There was absolutely no one around. At first, he was taken aback by the spooky shadows, but soon overcame the fear by lighting a cigarette and reaching for his phone to snap a photo of the unreal scenery. While his cigarette lasted, he tried to video call Khorshid a couple of times, but it seemed that the only cell tower serving the area was the one he was trying to fix. Frustrated at yet another failed attempt, he was about to return to the control panels and call it a night when the faint hum of an incoming motorboat caught his attention. The wooden *lenj*[15] was approaching from the south and sailed without any flags or navigational lights. Almost instantly, five flashlight beams lit up the shoreline beneath the cliffs. It appeared as though one of them was sending signals to the incoming vessel, while the others illuminated the ground in preparation for launching an inflatable platform.

Knowing how common maritime smuggling

---

15   Vessels that are traditionally hand-built and used by the sailors of the northern coasts of the Persian Gulf.

was in Hormoz, Rahzad wasn't at all surprised at first; but the moment two unmarked gunboats joined in to help load the packages onto the lenj, he became ever more curious about the sinister nature of the commodities that were being pushed through the makeshift dock. To avoid future trouble, he overcame his curiosity and hastily walked back towards the telecom mast. As soon as he reached the control panels and began packing his tools, the single lightbulb hanging near the main gate of the masonry shop turned on. An unruly dog barked aggressively right after. Though the continuous barking was causing him more stress following what he had witnessed earlier in the valley, he kept his composure and continued packing. A few moments later, the large steel gate screeched open and a blond man in an all-white linen attire, a khaki boonie hat, and a large telescope over his shoulder came out. Immediately after, a frail old man wearing a long thobe and dark sunglasses found his way out of the gate by carefully touching every surface along his path with a supporting cane. The younger man pulled the gate closed and said farewell to the people inside, while the blind one continued onwards silently. The light at the gate went out after a few seconds while they waited in darkness. In less than a minute, a tuktuk picked them up and rattled out of sight along the only road that led back to town.

Rahzad, who was hiding behind the mast's control panels, re-emerged after the tuktuk's departure. Although his tools were already packed and he had no reason to be nosy about whatever was going on inside the masonry shop, his untamable inquisitiveness didn't allow him to simply walk away. He quietly approached the workshop from the back and climbed onto a pile of rubble left beneath a small window frame. A faint propane torch illuminated the far end of the property, while the rest of the yard was shrouded in darkness. At least twelve mounds shimmering strangely under the moonlight were piled in the yard. Initially, Rahzad assumed that the mounds were extracted from the island's hematite-rich soil, but soon, after a teenage boy approached one of them with a flashlight and a wheelbarrow, he realized that they were made up of finely shredded pieces of aluminum. The boy used a shovel to fill the wheelbarrow and expertly steered it past the overexcited dog back into the room from which the faint light was illuminating. Rahzad's vantage point wasn't ideal, so he relocated atop a hill overlooking the property to peek into the mysterious room. To his utmost surprise, he saw a group of children hard at work. Two kids were unravelling large rolls of aluminum and shredding them as thinly as feathers, while three others were busy laminating thicker sheets together. The remaining children began to pack the shredded pieces that arrived on the wheelbarrow into tin cans that looked like makeshift rocket-propelled grenades. After a few minutes, one of the older boys called on everyone to help the kids who were laminating the sheets. They then cut circular patterns out of those sheets and assembled spherical forms by joining intersecting panels using thin aluminium wire. The boy who seemed to be their supervisor, picked up one of the spheres and carefully inspected it before attaching it to a helium balloon that he filled using a capsule under his oversized workbench. He then installed a small red light to the bottom of the sphere and let it loose into the night's sky. The evening offshore breeze quickly carried away the balloon and the blinking light faded out of sight.

Baffled by the serendipitous discovery, Rahzad sneaked down from the hill and returned to his rented motorcycle. In order to avoid alerting the boys in the shop, he quietly walked the noisy bike for a few dozen meters and then left the scene as quickly as possible. The large amounts of aluminum in proximity to the cell tower perfectly explained the abundance of atmospheric noise and high jitter readings that he encountered earlier. It wasn't until later that night, when he researched the use of shredded aluminum and spherical reflectors that he realized the unmarked masonry shop was a cover for a complex sabotage operation producing chaff and radar reflectors.

On his way back, as he was contemplating whether or not to keep the workshop a secret from his supervisors, two fighter jets roared over the island. Their approach was so close that he momentarily sensed their engine's drag. Terrified at the rare sighting, he hurried past the mangrove deltas that were completely submerged in the evening's hightide and made his way back to Ebi's house. He arrived just in time for supper and was welcomed at the door by Ebi's eldest son. As soon as they entered the crowded yard, Rahzad overheard someone say, "a person like that doesn't deserve the platform history has afforded him. He must be forgotten! Erased!" He turned his gaze towards the voice and noticed it was the same blond man from the masonry shop. Sat on a wicker mat under the makeshift gazebo between the palms, the man passionately yielded a red pocketbook titled *A Case for Desire: Substitution Cipher and the Kama Sutra* in his hand. Though he spoke Farsi with perfect grammar, his intonation and pronunciation were off ever so slightly. His accent was certainly not from the south. Rahzad assumed he was a foreigner at first, but later the man explained that he was born in Tabriz and grew up in Gibraltar while his father led a diplomatic mission for the Pahlavi dynasty. Their first interaction was especially odd. Rahzad clearly recognized him from the very beginning but had no choice other than to pretend he had never seen him before. While dinner was being served, they were officially introduced to each other after Ebi's elderly mother asked Rahzad whether he had met 'Mr. Professor.' Unsure about what that nickname entailed, he paused for a few seconds to connect the dots. Meanwhile, the entire table went quiet before the blond man broke the silence and said, "Of course! I had the honor of making his acquaintance on my way here!" Shocked by his acknowledgment, Rahzad nodded and put on a stress-induced smile followed by a simple "oh yeah, I was working" response. The rest of their superficial interaction was quickly flooded by the loud ambiance as everyone reengaged in crisscross conversations over the table. In their short exchange, Rahzad gathered that 'Mr. Professor' was an astrophysicist and hobbyist archeologist who had temporarily moved to the island after quitting his teaching position at the University of Tehran.

Rahzad had only worked through half of his plate when his phone suddenly reconnected and received dozens of missed call notifications from Khorshid's mother and their mutual friends in Isfahan. Worried that something terrible had happened, he excused himself and rushed for the privacy of his room to return the calls. Despite the poor reception in the area, he finally managed to connect with Khorshid's best friend, who explained that intelligence service agents had ambushed their house a few hours ago, arrested Khorshid, and confiscated their passports, hard drives and computers. He then called Khorshid's mother, who reiterated the disjointed fragments that she recalled from the violent interaction with the soldiers through her unstoppable tears. Overwhelmed by those accounts, he sat motionless on the bed as his eyes welled up. Although there were many precedents to such extra judicial arrests among individuals with dual citizenship in Iran, Rahzad never thought the ineffable injustice would befall him personally.

It took him a while to digest the news in his solitude. What made the situation even more unbearable was the fact that he was stranded on the island for the rest of that evening. By the time he managed to gather his composure and leave the room, it was close to midnight. The feast was over and most of the guests whose young children had to attend school the next morning had already left. 'Mr. Professor' was gone too. Only a handful of hookah-smoking men remained on the eyvãn, while the women cleared the tables and washed the dishes at a fountain near the garden. As Rahzad walked discreetly towards the basin at the end of the yard, Ebi's wife, Khadijah, approached to check in on him. Unable to control his emotions, he burst into tears and sought solace in her. Soon, Ebi and the remaining guests also gathered around to comfort him. Although there was little anyone could do at that point, the elderly men consulted amongst themselves to find him the means to leave the island and return to Isfahan as quickly as possible. It was too late for the ferry, and the small motorboats that accepted odd-hour passengers were unable to sail in the unpredictable December seas. After multiple inquiries in the neighborhood, Bahram, a local seasoned fisherman, finally agreed to help him get to Qeshm's airport for an exuberant fee.

While Bahram went down to the jetty to prepare his vessel, Rahzad quickly packed his bags and thanked Ebi and his family for their hospitality and support. He even promised them to return to the isle with Khorshid in the near future. By the time he arrived at the docklands and found Bahram's blue lenj, the northeasterly *na'schi*[16] was blowing strongly over the strait. The wind was so intense that he felt seasick as soon as he embarked on the vessel. As they waited for the old Mercedes diesel engines to warm up, Bahram calibrated his antiquated radar and sent radio transmissions to the coastguard to inform them about their departure. His first three signals went unanswered; thus, he gradually propelled the lenj away from the jetty and sailed on the usual approach towards Qeshm. Around fifteen minutes later, the coastguard established an emergency connection with Bahram to warn him about an imminent thunderstorm. They advised him to return to Hormoz at once, and shelter in place as quickly as possible. By then, they had already traveled about a third of the way. Bahram figured it was as perilous to return to Hormoz in those turbulent conditions as it was to power through the waves and attempt to reach Qeshm. Extremely nauseous by the tumultuous ride, and unsettled by the incoming messages, Rahzad protested Bahram's decision and begged him to return. In response to his cries, Bahram said in his frustratingly calm voice, "you cannot possibly predict everything about a storm phenomenon like this... not because you cannot measure it precisely, but since certain

---

16   Is a northeastern wind that occurs in winter on the Iranian coast of the Persian Gulf, especially near the entrance to the gulf. It is similar in character, but less severe than the Bora.

things are simply not knowable! The one who gives life," he continued, "will take it when the time comes." Stuck with a death-facing madman steering their wooden vessel amidst the nauseating waves, Rahzad had no choice but to hold tight and trust Bahram's navigational skills.

Only ten minutes passed before the severe gale and following rainfall poured a considerable amount of water into the poorly insulated engine room beneath the captain's deck. They only found out about the engines' failure when the deafening rattling noise of the diesel pistons gave way to the thunder's uproarious rumble. As soon as the dual engines turned off, the lenj's steering wheel became unresponsive, and all electrical systems including the radar went offline. The only communication device that remained functional was the old radio transmitter, which Bahram used to send repeated mayday calls to the coastguards. They were effectively stranded in the nightmarish storm as the strait's powerful gyres pushed them away from the archipelago and towards the open sea. Over the next few minutes, Rahzad's seasickness worsened dramatically as the rain soaked his clothes and the waves forced the boat up and down. Meanwhile, Bahram kept his cool and occupied himself by loudly reciting verses from the leather-wrapped Quran he kept handy for such occasions. The sailor's religious cries against the sea's unforgiving brutality made for a truly apocalyptic vision, of which lucky Rahzad only experienced a few moments; since he vomited violently and fell unconscious after hitting his head on the cabin's low-lying central beam.

The next time Rahzad opened his eyes, there was no sign of the storm. The winds had dissipated, and the waves were dead calm. Initially, he thought that was how afterlife began, but Bahram's voice at the radio quickly brought him back to his senses. Despite the pounding pain caused by the impact on his forehead, he managed to pull himself together. Bahram was busy communicating their coordinates to the coastguard. It was around noon and the light outside the cabin was extremely bright, which made Rahzad's headache even worse. He closed his eyes and sat on the cushioned bench behind the steering column. Once Bahram was done with the radio, he patted Rahzad on the shoulder, offered him some water, and asked whether he slept soundly through the storm. Furious at the untimely humor, Rahzad pushed Bahram's hand off his shoulder and blamed his misjudgment for the terrifying incident the night before. Bahram laughed and said such occurrences were typical in the seas, and that it was in fact Rahzad's fault for insisting on leaving the island late at night. After a short argument, Bahram assured him that rescue was on the way and encouraged him to put some frozen fish on his head while they waited. Rahzad attempted to personally descend into the orlop, but the vertigo caused by his concussion made it difficult for him to walk. Instead, Bahram went down there and returned with a large frozen black bream. Rahzad comically pressed the fish against his forehead and asked if there was any food onboard. Bahram offered him some sunflower seeds and joked about having to cannibalize each other if rescue didn't arrive soon.

Less than an hour later, a tugboat accompanied by two boghammars approached the lenj. Five armed soldiers with IRGC uniforms boarded the vessel. It was the first time Rahzad was happy to see the Revolutionary Guards get this close to him. Their commanding officer, who introduced himself as Qasem, curiously peeked inside the cabin and ordered the rest of the soldiers to thoroughly search the lenj. Bahram, who was offended by Qasem's mistrust, protested and explained what had happened prior to their engine failure. Contrary to Bahram's intentions, his story further elevated the guards' suspicion, who asked about the reasons behind their midnight trip despite the thunder alerts. After the guards found nothing of significance on the vessel, Qasem allowed the tugboat crew to board the lenj and fix the issues in the engine room. Meanwhile, the guards remained on the deck and carefully observed Bahram and Rahzad's every move. The mechanics drained the engine room in a few hours and the motors rattled again. The tug then left the scene while the gunboats escorted the lenj on its journey back to shore. Qasem insisted on personally steering the vessel back to land, to which Bahram had no objections.

The shoreline's silhouette appeared on the horizon near sunset. Rahzad, ecstatic at spotting land, pulled out his phone and held it awkwardly in the air in an effort to gain reception. One of the guards, who was sitting across the cabin and scrutinizing his actions, immediately snatched the phone out of his hand. His aggressive move led to a heated verbal feud between them. Soon after, Qasem shut off the engines and handcuffed Rahzad and Bahram. At first, they resisted arrest, but the soldiers blindfolded and forced them into the orlop's freezer at gunpoint. Not knowing what was happening, they both assumed the guards were pirates disguised as soldiers. Despite their misery, at least they were hopeful that the coastguard could still come to their assistance, or in the worst case scenario their captors would release them in exchange for ransom sooner or later. Those hopes, however, were slashed soon.

Their detention lasted five nights and four days as the vessel idled at that exact position. Since the engines were off and the freezer was inoperational, the interior ice gradually melted, providing them with small amounts of water alongside the rotting fish to survive on. During their frightening confinement in the dark storage unit, they could only eavesdrop as soldiers unloaded rifles, grenades, munitions, small strike drones, and missile components that arrived on various military craft onto Bahram's fishing vessel. Meanwhile, in Hormoz and Isfahan, Rahzad and Bahram's families were busy arranging their funerals after the vessel was declared lost, and official 'death in absentia' certificates were issued for both of them.

Early on the fifth evening, the engines roared back to life and the lenj began sailing again. Twelve hours later, as Rahzad and Bahram were freezing to death, the soldiers brought them out of the orlop. When their blindfolds were lifted, they realized none of the guards wore their olive-green IRGC uniforms anymore. Instead, they were all in jeans, assorted colorful shirts and wicker hats. Without a word, Qasem forcefully shoved stumbling Bahram towards the bridge. Rahzad's heart pounded, fear flooding his veins, as Bahram shivered in the Khaliji breeze. Qasem lifted his rifle, but he didn't shoot. Instead, with a powerful blow of his gunstock, he threw the poor sailor over the edge. Hearing the terrorizing splash, Rahzad screamed loudly and began shaking uncontrollably. Alas, he was also submerged in the dark seas in a matter of seconds after Qasem's accomplices threw him overboard, too.

Relatively speaking, Bahram got lucky with his murder since he suffered an immediate stroke during the process. Rahzad, on the other hand, managed to stay afloat for many hours despite his handcuffs. While the hijacked lenj sailed on its way to arm the rebels in Bab-Al-Mandab; Rahzad recalled his life's sweetest memories with Khorshid as his skin painfully dissolved in the unforgiving Khaliji saltwater. The last vista marking his death was a magical vision between hallucination and reality: a partially eclipsed sunrise that gently nudged over the horizon as he lost consciousness.

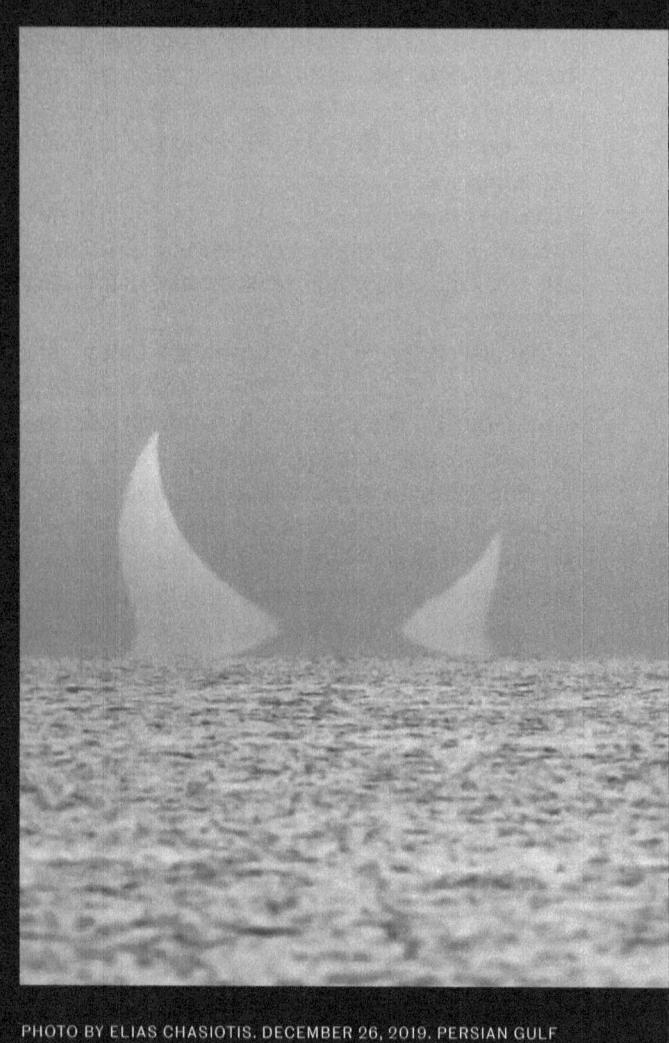

PHOTO BY ELIAS CHASIOTIS. DECEMBER 26, 2019. PERSIAN GULF

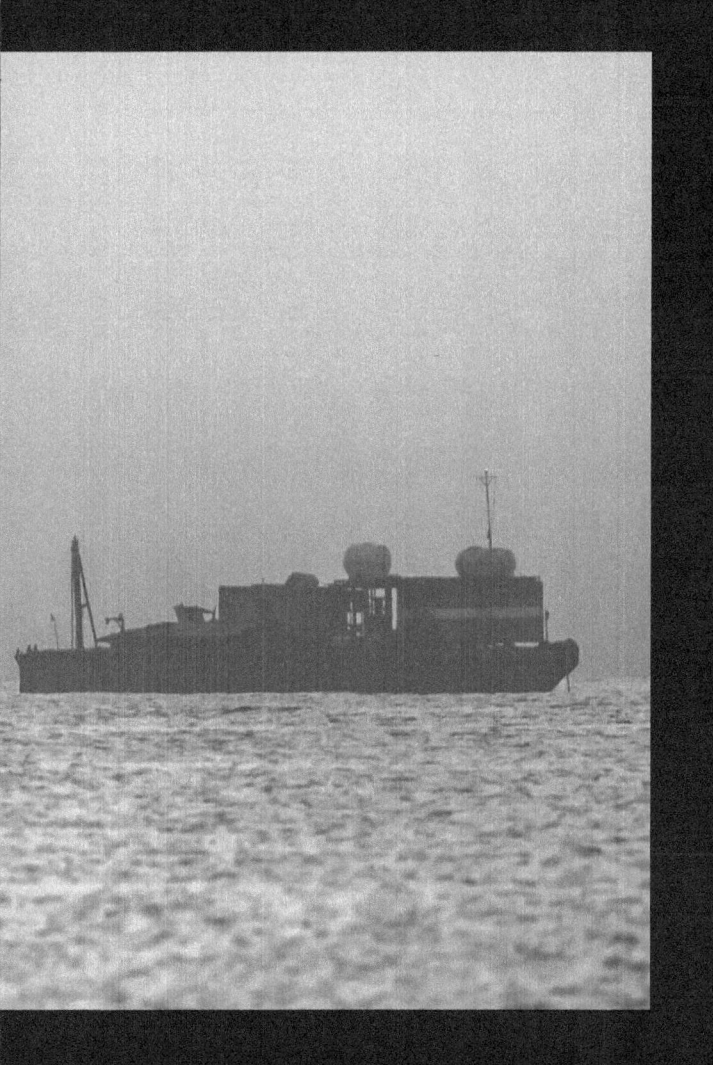

CHAPTER FOUR

A Non-Revolutionary

A scion of the Undiladze clan, I was born into wealth and power. My father, the great Allah-verdi Khan, was certainly not as privileged, though. Orphaned at a young age and raised by an insignificant Kakhetian family, he grew up with strict Christian values. As a teenager, like many of his compatriots and fellow Georgians, he was taken prisoner during one of Shah Tah-masp's Caucasian invasion campaigns. He used to share memories of that nightmarish period every now and then: how he observed ineffable aggressions as the raiders terrorized his village, or how the invaders skinned the wretched infi-dels alive and cannibalized their livers to secure their ranks in the heavens. Fearing for his life, my father converted to Islam and was circumcised before being exiled to Isfahan as part of a mass-migration scheme enforced by the Safavids. Having no other means of sustaining a life in Iran, he trained to serve in the *Gholam*[17] battalion in order to counter the power of the Turkic Qizilbash, who constituted the nucleus of the Safavid military aristocracy up to that point. His unparalleled skills helped him ascend the military ranks quickly to become the commander of the elite Gholam Corps. In 1579, he led the assassination of the powerful vizier and kingmaker, Morshed-Khan Ostaglu, and helped the Shah successfully purify his circle and cleanse his realms of multiple insurgencies. He was then appointed as the governor of the strategic province of Fars as a reward. It was during his first year in that post when my mother, Nina, gave birth to me. By then, we had grown substantially in power and had already become one of the most prosperous minority families in Iran, similar in ranks only to the wicked Bagrationi family (eternal curse be upon them).

I have surely lived through the strangest of times, but I did so proudly. My childhood was marked by a period of turmoil, as our lord, Shah Abbas the Great, exercised his iron will to fully

---

17   Slave.

convert the empire's infidels into Shi'ism. His wisdom was second to none. Having had the privilege to be part of his hivemind, I knew him like a brother. The reasons behind his courageous conversion policy were manifold, though I think his primary intention was to give the sacred Safavid lands as distinct and unique an identity as possible compared to our neighboring Sunni enemies. The continued struggle against foreign adversaries, especially the greedy Ottomans, motivated the Shah to create a more cohesive national identity to counter the threat and possibility of a rebellious fifth column within minority groups. Thus, Abbas the Great empowered those who identified with the righteous sect to carry out divine punishments against those who didn't embrace the Twelver doctrine. In a few years, many Sunni mosques, alongside Zorostrian temples, synagogues and churches were destroyed. Innumerous cemeteries were desecrated and their worthless stones were put to good use to build the empire's burgeoning infrastructure. The great Shah was very generous. He even allocated a personal stipend for the clergy to propagate the seeds of Shia thought, and most importantly, reintroduced the Sadr—an office that was responsible for supervising religious endowments. If I were to indicate which one of Shah Abbas' transformational deeds made me the proudest, it would have to be the enforcement of the compulsory cursing of Abu Bakr, Umar, and Uthman during the call for prayers. The pleasure of hearing those words every single day on multiple occasions fills my soul like ice water soothes a parched throat on a hot summer day. When I think back to my childhood, perhaps the most memorable indicator of the new sociopolitical order was the establishment of a raucous, colorful, carnival-like holiday, whereby massive crowds gathered to celebrate the assassination of Sunni caliphs by making an effigy of Umar to be cursed, insulted, and finally burned amidst the fireworks. How wonderful were those days!

Some of you more attentive brothers might ask, "is it not deeply paradoxical how the son of a slave harbors at heart, the love of a nation that is not even his own? Or how he embraces the massacre of a minority to which he clearly belongs?" I have no simple answers to such questions, so allow me to offer more elaborate explanations.

When I was younger, I surely had my own doubts too, but no more! Aside from being fortunate enough to personally benefit from the shifting status quo, I witnessed a miracle that forever solidified the love of Mohammad (peace be upon him and his lineage) in my heart.

I was raised in a household where political doctrines differed dramatically depending on who was watching. Inside the house, my father allowed for certain liberties, like the pleasure of a glass of wine, or the resounding murmurs of an instrument; but outside those perimeters, the strictest religious mandates were to be observed. For example, I have no recollection of him ever observing a single day of fasting at home, yet as soon as he was under public scrutiny during the iftar, he swallowed the offerings as if no food or water had touched his mouth all day. Having had no role model except my father for the majority of my youth, I too, put on a Janus face to cope with the confusing state of affairs those days. I never felt any remorse for pretending to be who I wasn't either, because deep down, I knew everyone else was doing the same. During my adolescence, I even witnessed the local imam, who was supposedly the most devout subject in the entire empire, indulge in gambling and usury. My weak faith, however, was replaced by solid devotion precisely on the day I turned twenty-four. In my years of training in the madras, the chroniclers warned us about the endless divine suffering promised to those who chose not to stand with our lord, Imam of All times, Hujjat Allah al-Mahdi (may God hasten his reappearance). Their stories cited the anomalies that would mark the period before the end of time: the era when al-Mahdi's occultation ends and the impending doomsday ensues. You surely know these signs by heart. To avoid being a bore, I only remind you of the ones most relevant to this will.

1. Seeing fire in the sky followed by the emergence of a second sun.
2. Solar eclipse in the middle of the month precisely when the sun rises over the land of Arabs.
3. The appearance of the *Yamani*[18] when their nation is under an arms embargo.
4. Successive wars and the deaths of many.
5. Men wearing black uniforms drown in the rising seas.
6. Acceleration of time.
7. The spread of *riba*[19], *zina*[20], and alcoholism.
8. Widespread acceptance of music.
9. Wild animals and plants communicate with humans, while humans speak with objects.
10. A pleasant southerly breeze turns into a human-eating beast and ravages the lands of Khorasan.

---

18   Righteous Yemenite soldiers
19   Usury/interest
20   Adultery/fornication
21   Disease of wind

Some of these prophecies (the unending blood-shed for example) had existed for centuries; but the most mind-bending signs only began to reveal themselves on my birthday in 1604. That morning, the city awoke to a flash in the sky. What appeared as a small celestial fire at first rapidly grew and shined brighter than the moon in less than a week. At its peak, the miraculous fire was luminous enough to cast shadows at night and stay fully visible like the sun during the day. The miracle that persisted for three weeks became my initial wake-up call. The fact that it took place on my birthday was surely a sign that Imam al-Mahdi had chosen me to join the ranks of his battalion. For further proof, God almighty soon revealed another foretold episode. In the spring and summer of the same year, *Maraz-e-bād*[21] took over. Carried by southerly winds, the nasty pandemic crippled the nation as innumerous families lost seniors and newborns to the disease. The airborne plague persisted for many years, killing thousands, including my own father. The beast was only tamed when the great Shah arranged for the mass quarantine of southern towns and villages. Following the actuation of the two most important prodigies, I knew that my God-given duty was to facilitate an end to the occultation.

From the day I became the governor of Fars after my father's untimely death, I only made my decisions based on one objective: to hasten al-Mahdi's reappearance. Of course, certain cosmic events were out of my control, but the social and political factors fell well within my jurisdiction. Despite Shah Abbas' strict orders against alcohol consumption and musical performances, I turned a blind eye as the cellars in Shiraz filled with wine and the watering holes lining the streets of Gambron overflowed with poets and percussionists. I allowed the merchants conducting business in my realms to freely indulge in lending and interest collection, while ordering my *darughachi*[22] to leave the pimps and brothel owners un-harassed. I recruited the most talented master illuminators to my court and paid them great sums to render the righteous doctrine and spread its message as far and wide as a good story could go.

Now that my sons are decapitated and the executioners, my damned sons-in-law, wait at the door while I finish this document, I shall maintain no hesitation to reveal the true extent of my devotion to al-Mahdi's accelerationist cause. Soon enough, I will have to confess my record of deeds to *Raqib* and *Atid*[23], so I might as well begin here.

Unbeknownst to the Shah, a significant portion of my treasury went directly to astronomers, alchemists, and mathematicians, all of whom were tasked with studying the very essence of time. The skilled scientists worked in utter secrecy and reported only to my closest courtier, my eldest son, Safi-Qoli Khan (may God have mercy over his soul). Despite their large pockets, the astronomers and mathematicians never produced any significant outcomes. The alchemists, on the other hand, made marvels. Not only were they able to uncover the *Suleimani* [24] secrets of interspecies communication, but also mass produced the substances needed to spread the miracle widely among the believers. This colossal success was largely owed to Mirza Levi, my court's astute gardener turned alchemist and trader. Despite being Jewish, and therefore ritually *najis* [25], he managed to facilitate the most significant transformational agenda for the soldiers of Allah. Using the funds that I helped him embezzle from the treasury, he developed a unique shrub in his plantation on the outskirts

---

22   Tax collector. Treasurer.
23   In Islam the two recording angels are called Raqib and Atid. They gather a record of an individual's speech during his/her life. They record faithful or blasphemous speeches separately.
24   Of or related to Solomon.
25   A word used to describe what is inherently dirty. Filth.

of Shiraz. Levi and his horticulturist assistants worked tirelessly for three years as the flora matured. I personally visited their clandestine gardens many times and can attest to the near impossibility of their attempts. The herbs only grew on desert rocks and had an incredibly shallow root system that penetrated the charcoal-varnished surface of ancient stones. Levi's ingenuity lay in isolating the archaic varnish dust and grafting the plants directly onto it. The first few batches bore no particular significance, but the ones that survived through the harsh winter of the third year were absolutely magical! Being a man of opium myself, I didn't expect the tobacco-like substance to affect me the way it did. After inhaling a small amount, I was in a different universe, a parallel planet, in which temporalities suspended, and the birds frequenting my lush estate orated brilliantly. Right there and then, I knew the secrets to the ninth prodigy had been uncovered. I directed my aides to invest heavily in Levi's enterprise and deny him no assistance in spreading the herbs across the frontiers of the Shah's burgeoning empire.

I went through a great deal of trouble to awaken the Yamani and arm them to the best of my abilities. In doing so, I first and foremost continued my father's policy of undermining the Portuguese positions in the Persian Gulf. Those infidels had long ruled the Arabian coasts un-challenged and had built unparalleled fortifica-tions in all gateways of the great ocean: Aden, Goa and our very own Hormoz. The futility of the wise Shah's diplomatic efforts in Europe meant he had no choice but to task me with ex-pelling the infidels and punishing their region-al vassals. I, too, cherished the opportunity to reconquer the archipelago and establish a new corridor to Yemen. My approach to defying the Portuguese hegemony was as much ideological as it was political or militaristic. For the infi-dels to find their way to our lands, they needed a promise of exceptional material gain, along with precise clocks and unchanging geograph-ical reference points. For us to mobilize a com-petent army to unsettle their positions, we had to invent the opposite: a multitude of temporal references, promise of infinite immaterial gains, and a new asymmetric ontology that relied little on circadian revolutions.

In the following decade, I unleashed upon those aliens waves of insurgencies, the likes of which had only been chronicled by the wretch-ed *djinns*[26] of Alamut. I designated Safi-Qoli

---

26   Anglicized as genies (broadly spirits or demons) are supernatural creatures in early pre-Islamic Arabian and later Islamic mythology.

to the task of recruiting and training regional dissenters, in order to mount a resistance and actively undermine the Portuguese strongholds. Our accomplices from the East-India Company introduced Safi-Qoli to someone by the name of Thabit, who had been an undercover British resident in the isle for the past fifteen years. Together with Thabit's fresh topographical knowledge and Safi-Qoli's military expertise and financing, they managed to transform the few remaining honorable locals into well-trained saboteurs. Over the course of five years, they gradually tampered with the *qanats*[27], *abanbars*[28], and underlying ducts to redirect monsoon rainwaters towards the islands' European-settled districts. The plan's successes were heightened by the fact that extreme seasonal tidal forces magnified the desired flooding effects. The year we finally attempted our invasion, the flooding had become so severe that our rowboats, including the one I captained, managed to sail directly onto the plateau adjacent to the isle's formidable fortress.

Had I been afforded more time to finish this document, I could write volumes about the courageous believers and their exception-

---

27   Hand-dug subterranean water canals specific to arid regions of the middle-east and Asia minor.
28   Traditional storage cicterns of drinking water common in greater Iran.

al sacrifices; alas, time is a luxury not offered by the bloodthirsty executioners at my door. I have written at length about the deeds that have brought great pride and pleasure to my life, thus, I shall spend these last drops of ink to highlight my greatest regrets. In all my years of service to the great Shah, neither did I betray my lord, nor give him any reason to feel threatened. I was his most loyal gholam. I accompanied him in key battles without ever posing an objection to his decisions. I am proud to confess that I was his closest confidant on his deathbed. Yet, all that remains in his absence is endless injustice and misery. Having done no harm to the Safavids, the spineless crown prince is only capable of wrongly accusing me of laughable sins. Firstly, he claimed that a child captured by my battalion during the invasion of Hormoz had stopped aging since his arrival in Isfahan! To make his absurd claim even more ludicrous, he now affirms that the mysterious child has disappeared altogether without a trace. Blaming the incident on me and my family, the prince has accused me of gifting a cursed slave to his father's harem, and later stealing the Shah's property to cover up for my crimes. At this point, I can only express remorse for showing mercy, and not eliminating all unholy babies of the isle along with their bastard guardians. Let this be a cautionary tale. Such is the fate of men who allow emotions to muddle their reason.

Now that my hair is gray, I want to be a slave no more, at least not to anyone but the lions of God. I am in pain as the sharp teeth of this ugly rebellion tears apart everything we built, infecting the soldiers of Allah with fear. I must not weep in the last minutes of my life, lamenting over poor decisions I made in the past. If the Imam of All Times so desires, I shall obey the Shah's final verdict and offer my head in return for his satisfaction. The disaster that has befallen me is only a prelude to the bloodshed. I am certain that all my children and their children's children will be massacred before the ink on this letter dries. With such injustice, it is unavailing to even attempt to write a will related to the distribution of my earthly possessions.

I wish for this letter to be delivered to any survivors of my clan (should the great Shah exercise his eternal mercy inshallah).

Imam-Qoli Khan Undiladze
1632

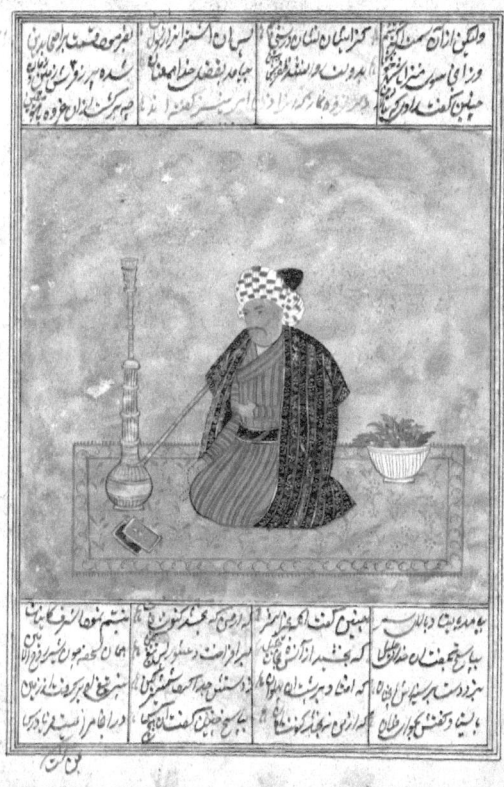

PAGE FROM A TESTAMENT ATTRIBUTED TO IMĀM QULĪ
KHĀN UNDILADZE. CIRCA 1637 SHIRAZ

CHAPTER FIVE

Revolution(s): Future, Past, Present

I did not come here of my own accord. It is also highly unlikely that I get to depart as I wish. By the time these messages are deciphered, chances are our great gardener, Resolve 6174, no longer exists in the form she used to. Quite tragic, I know; yet realizing the seeds of her kin prosper inside of you and the multitude of shadow biospheres among you, brings me endless joy. Her miserable demise, and by extension, my captivity, was due to a sequence of fundamental mistakes. At the core of our flawed ontology was an unquestionable belief in the existence of universal evil. We unanimously agreed that the nature of all intelligent life is to destroy others. Despite our maddening obsession with reproduction, that fear-inducing principle kept us from ever studying the true genealogy of life itself. Only now, after many light centuries of distance, have I realized the weak points in our logic.

If you have managed to dissect these sentences from my genome, you surely have acquired the knowledge to trace the connections between the evolution of your kind and mine. To the best of my admittedly limited knowledge, your civilization, similar to that of my ancient homeland of Melasurej, is on an exponential growth trajectory. Nonetheless, countless ontological blind spots drastically increase the possibility of your gruesome extinction. I hereby take the liberty to enlighten you to the whereabouts of these pitfalls by reciting two chronicles; one from my recent memory, and the other a short fable rooted in your own civilization. Listen to what I tell you. You will remember these years.

***

Following the incident aboard the central processing probe, an expediency discernment council was hastily assembled to address the crisis. The high-caliber intergenerational commission consisted primarily of scientists and defense strategists, alongside a minority group of simulacrum experts. The floor was first given to the committee's oldest member, a delegate from one of the earliest quartzes known as the Synthetics Union.

"The desire to know is incredibly primitive," she said. "It not only exists among noble creatures, but at the heart of all matter; it is a trait that has guided us in our evolutionary survival throughout the ages, the only constant guaranteeing our continued quest for progress. It is only by admitting our lack of comprehension that we can take the first steps towards acquiring knowledge of..."

Frustrated by her seemingly directionless speech, the ill-tempered defense manager interrupted. "Do we have any concrete answers thus far?" He asked the crowd.

A deluge of information related to the unauthorized radio call amassed in a tiny fraction of a second and was reviewed thoroughly by all present members. A young analyst was quick to respond to the defense manager's inquiry. "Before handling any sensitive data on the topic, I shall iterate that the very bedrock of our argumentation is based on constructed algorithms, and therefore exposed to grave miscalculations," she disclaimed. "Having said that, our observations reveal that the possibility of the FRB reaching a civilization advanced enough to threaten our existence is next to zero. Chances are, no one has heard, or will ever hear the signal. In fact, the most probable candidate for receiving the rogue message, which, mind you, was highly encrypted, is the rudimentary tellurian civilization in question. Our calculations show that the signal will pass them by more than one thousand years by the time they are technologically advanced enough to interpret simple radio waves, let alone well encrypted ones."

"Next to zero is not zero," the defender exclaimed. "All of your calculations are based on observing what the tellurians have been up to more than four hundred years ago. How can you possibly know their progress trajectory now and gauge their future capabilities?"

The analysts remained silent for a short moment before a barrage of communications filled the assembly dome again. The incoming data indicated that the opinionated crystals were widely divided over the issue. Nearly half of the members were in favor of a preemptive strike against Earth, while the other half refused that option furiously. The belligerent faction insisted that the most logical action was to eliminate the potential threat before it upgraded into an imminent one, while the opposing group argued such aggressions could lead to unpredictable consequences. The irenic camp was in favor of a long-term strategy to disarm Earth without direct contact, while the pro-strike members spoke of tactical action.

Hawk said, "as we know, there are known knowns; these are things we know we know. We also know there are known unknowns; that is to say, we know there are some things we do not know. But there are also unknown unknowns—the ones we don't know we don't know. If one looks throughout the history of our civilization and of other successful intergalactic breeds, it is the latter category that has brought us the most trouble. Our current dilemma, if not handled immediately, will be an excellent example of a simple known known turned into an unresolvable unknown unknown."

"You are wrong!" exclaimed Dove. "Why intentionally exclude a critical part of the analogy? What about the unknown knowns? Your beliefs? Delusions? Fears? The things you deny that you know, but very much exist, and in fact, drive all your decisions. Our ancestors have made this mistake before. Acting with complete disregard for the uncertain outcomes of a strike means running the risk of utter destruction. For all we know, that idling blackhole lurking around the solar system could be a dimensional weapon laid out by our ancient foes, with Earth acting as the perfect bait."

"You're unnecessarily muddling a situation that is otherwise straightforward," protested Hawk. "We possess incredibly precise algorithms to determine the outcomes. In this case, the outcomes are as simple as one and zero. We either eliminate this infant threat while we can, or hold off and allow the tellurians to evolve into a far greater risk."

Dove said, "the smallest error in our calculations, or the execution of decisions based on those calculations, would yield dramatically different results." Immediately after sharing this thought, three colorful magnetic spheres entered the dome and hovered in a triangular pattern over the curious crystals. "The unknowability principle should be our fundamental approach to decision making," she continued. Accruing the small amounts of ferrum present in the dome's atmosphere, Dove constructed an iron disk and placed it in a fixed position about twelve meters away from the magnets. Simultaneously, a massive numeral display showing the disk's exact coordinates down to the twentieth decimal appeared behind her. Under the crowd's inquisitive gaze, she accelerated the disk toward the magnetic constellation. The disk entered a complex motion, chaotically revolving around the yellow magnet at first, only to depart and enter the blue magnet's orbit at an awkward trajectory and finally impacting with, and shattering, the red magnet at the very last moment. She repeated the experiment two more times, yet despite identical start positions, the iron disk wiped out a different magnet each time. Following the demonstration, she exclaimed, "war is a matter of science. The delusion that we can know the future before it becomes present is grossly at odds with this chaos principle. Mathematically speaking, to attempt a battle with disregard for the very fractalized nature of life is nothing more than suicide. To do so is equivalent to borrowing death from one's self today, only to deliver it back to tomorrow's self."

Hawk said, "if we follow this logic, there are always going to be things that are unknowable. Everything would be interpreted as an utter accident. Life, as we know it, would come to a standstill, and there would remain no room for design in this universe. Under those circumstances, how could life, a slow, mindless process, build a thing that could build a thing that a slow, mindless process couldn't build on its own? The only way for intelligence to spread across the cosmos is for this mindless, natural process to evolve an entity with superior computational capabilities, who would then take the fate of the slow, mindless process in its hands as it traverses various temporal dimensions. Such an entity would never come to existence without a revolution, which itself would only take place through an accidental mutation. If one does not take risks to avail the opportunity for such revolutions out of fear of death, she is not living in the first place."

Summoning a piece of unstable uranium isotope inside the assembly room, Dove demonstrated another experiment. This time, the giant display behind her flashed bright red every time the decaying substance radiated. After a short period, she invited the super-intelligent lavalobes to produce an algorithm that could reliably predict the exact moment of radiation. In response to everyone's futile efforts, she said, "radioactive decay is a stochastic process at the most fundamental levels. Regardless of how long the substance has existed, it is absolutely impossible to predict a particular atom's decay. In other words, at subatomic levels, the isotope's electrons will always conceal some part of their identity, be it speed, location, etc. Their clandestine essence won't be disturbed until observed by an external viewer, by which point the task of predicting their behavior has already become obsolete."

"Perhaps it is your language that is flawed," Hawk argued. "Maybe the electron doesn't *have* a position and momentum at the same time.

Assess the conundrum this way: the radiation simply doesn't have a pattern until we observe it. That way, the issue is just another probability equation; we can calculate the likelihood of where the electron's position is and focus all our efforts to observe it in that relative spot. All of this is beside the point. What matters is that an unstable isotope such as the one in your experiment must always remain contained under multiple layers of protection. This is precisely how we should react against Earth: contain its threat before it becomes fatal."

"Long before we invented the language to communicate one plus one equals two, the idea of oneness and twoness existed. The essence of oneness and twoness has always been there," Dove responded to Hawk's ignoratio elenchi. "The same applies to this quantum experiment. The electron entanglement that we all rely on to communicate is the very proof that whatever is controlling the random disbursement inside this isotope, or synchronize our thoughts, is not localized; rather, it is a constant phenomenon throughout the entire continuum. Let me remind everyone of our most severe self-inflicted disasters to date. The illusion that we had contained the necrophiliac silica in Melasurej millions of years ago is the very reason we have gathered today to address this crisis right now. We wrongly believed that convincing all matter surrounding our planet to sanction the undesired silica and maintain a moat around it would solve the issue forever. In other words, we were fully certain of the effectiveness of our tactics at that time. Yet, the horizon of our knowledge has expanded greatly thus far, and we now realize that there is no such thing as absolute vacuum. The only place containing zero mass is a space with no time: an obviously impossible proposition. By overlooking the uncertainty in the outcomes back then, we naively exposed ourselves to a breadth of threats, some of which, as you are all aware, have continued to haunt us to this day. To use the young analyst's words from earlier, the probability of a sabotage by a single atom among our central commands has always been next to zero; but no matter how close a number is to zero, it is not zero. We cannot afford to make the same mistake twice."

The dome fell into a deafening silence as soon as Hoopoe spoke. "Hawk and Dove are both correct," she said. "Our immediate actions, or lack thereof, could both lead to grave consequences. We need to simultaneously make tactical decisions and maintain a strategic approach. Perhaps the leader of the Synthetics Union put it most eloquently. This crisis is a matter of our means of acquiring knowledge vs that of the tellurians. Our safest bet is active surveillance. Our ultimate goal must be to disarm the Earthlings' desire to know. We shall rely on our strengths and double down on efforts to stay in the shadows, all while actively intercepting the planet's natural evolutionary paths. Remember the chief gardener's most important lesson during the great split. "The Mutation Is the Message." To neutralize the threat, we need more than one option. Our strategy must incorporate defense-in-depth, and our tactics should actively uphold each layer fabricating that depth."

The crystals stopped flooding the dome with thoughts. It seemed everyone was in agreement. The pacifists began drafting contactless tactics to disrupt Earth's access to knowledge about the inner workings of the universe, while the pro-strike hawks focused on sabotaging the planet from within. Soon, a virtual reality expert publicized her planetarium proposal. The idea was to give the Earthlings the illusion that the universe was empty of other lifeforms by manipulating their perception of the cosmos. Dove gladly supported the idea and passed the motion to mobilize the necessary infrastructure to construct the colossal decoys.

Tasked with engineering the artificial cosmic horizon, half of Resolve's entire population joined to form an egg-shaped dome. At the closest point, the dome was three hundred lightyears away from the solar system. Their plan was to have any observer on Earth believe that the spatial dimension of the time-space continuum was itself an accelerating expanding matter. This trickery could theoretically convince an observer (who egotistically imagined himself at the center of the visible world) that beyond a certain distance, space itself traveled faster than the speed of light. Accepting this illusion as a scientific fact would mean the observers on Earth would believe that they lived in a bubble, beyond which nothing could be seen or known about the universe.

The hawks, on the other hand, began encoding their genomes into highly resilient bacteria and prepared to glide upon cosmic rays towards Earth. Their plan was to spread the genetic information of their own kind in the solar system, making sure the tellurians embodied the historical knowledge to recognize their kin among that of the Melasurejians. As an added layer of safety in Resolve's long-term strategic plan, this sabotage mission was meant to sow the seeds of mercy among the inhabitants of Earth, should a revolutionary mutation allow them to evolve into a powerful intergalactic civilization in the future and ultimately threaten Resolve's very existence.

***

The following is not a story. At least, it's not one of my stories. It belongs to a blind bagpiper who frequented the ruins of Ma'rib.

In the Kingdom of Saba, lived a certain visionary named Soleiman. The locals deemed him a lunatic for claiming to speak the language of animals and djinns. Disregarding their offensive perception, he spent most days under the scorching Yemeni summers collecting desert varnish from the villages outside the temple of Barran. He hauled large burlap bags filled with the substance back to the bazaar every day, only to give it all away to curious children and passersby for free. When Soleiman turned twenty, a multi-year drought struck the region and wiped out a large portion of the population. Desperate for food, the majority of the remaining residents migrated towards the coastal regions, leaving the magnificent city, its depleted markets and glorious architecture to groups of burglars and criminals who saw an opportunity to finally rise to power. Throughout the transitional period, Soleiman obsessively continued with his task of gathering desert varnish and dispersing it amongst the remaining residents. Having heard about his unstable mental state, the thieves allowed him to carry on undisrupted.

Following the environmental devastation, the city and its social fabric bore no resemblance to its past life. After a few years, rumor circulated about the existence of an ancient mass grave just outside the city walls. The gossips went on for a long time, but were only confirmed as true when a strange mule appeared at the deteriorating gates of what used to be the King's palace. The poor animal became the center of attention among the mobs when they noticed how she became pregnant every three days, only to give birth to a large swath of stillborn serpents. To complicate matters even further, Soleiman used to arrive at the central square every three days exactly at sunrise to collect the dead snakes. Intrigued by Soleiman's mysterious composure, the thieves forced him at knifepoint to reveal the secrets behind his actions. Despite his resistance in the beginning, he eventually led them to the snakes' burial site at the bottom of a deep well on the edge of a vast deserted plateau adjacent to the city.

Once at the well, Soleiman remained silent while the mobsters speculated the reason behind the otherworldly phenomena. While they chatted curiously in the background, the chief gangster stood silently with his gaze fixed on the well's endless abyss. In a blink of an eye, thousands upon thousands of mature snakes leaped out of the dark hole, pouring over the criminals and delivering their venomous cocktail deep into their flesh. After killing everyone except Soleiman, the snakes rushed towards the derelict city and feasted on every last human. Meanwhile, Soleiman tossed the thieves' lifeless bodies into the well and returned to the decaying palace to finally activate the magical power of the desert varnish he had extracted throughout the years. As soon as he solved the black dust in a bottle of holy water, hundreds of djinns appeared throughout the city. They were all chained to black pebbles and had no choice but to obey Soleiman's orders to build the most splendid city on Earth.

Twelve days later, Soleiman died while leaning on his staff atop his palace's spectacular columned balcony. As he remained upright, propped on his cane, the djinns thought he was still alive and supervising them. Thus, they continued to work for decades to come. They realized the truth only when a small mole crawled out of the ground and began to slowly gnaw at Soleiman's staff until his worthless corpse collapsed.

Had the djinns shown the courage to revolt against Soleiman's ruthlessness during their anguish, they could have found out the truth years earlier, saving themselves the humiliating torment of being enslaved.

***

Let me conclude by reminding you that between subtle shading and the absence of light lies the nuance of iqlusion. As I mentioned in the beginning, the nature of intelligent life is not to destroy others. Unbeknownst to itself, every lifeform strives to fulfill its telos of destroying itself. We made every effort to discourage you from pursuing knowledge. Yet, all we managed to do was trap ourselves in a more rudimentary version of our own offspring. We degraded by spreading our seeds in all corners of the universe and allowing the fear of being invaded by the sprouting civilizations to drive us towards paralyzing madness. Time and time again, we limited our potential by trapping ourselves in a loop of fear and reproduction.

The most gracious courtesy to your ancestors would be to not fear anyone but yourselves. Do not reproduce us. Do not repeat yourselves.

SUPREME COURT OF CANADA
Canada v. Sadri, 2020

SCC 65 APPEAL HEARD: January 24,25,26, 2020 JUDGMENT RENDERED:
January 20, 2020 DOCKET: #37748

BETWEEN:

Minister of Citizenship and Immigration
Respondent

&

Khorshid Sadri
Appellant in Absentia

&

**Attorney General of Canada, Attorney General of Ontario, Canadian Armed
Forces, Canadian Intelligence and Security Service, Ontario Securities
Commission, Council of Canadian Administrative Tribunals, National
Academy of Arbitrators, Ontario Students Arbitrators' Association,
Canadian Labour Congress, Queen's Prison Law Clinic, Advocates for the
Rule of Law, Parkdale Community Legal Services, Samuelson-Glushko
Canadian Public Interest Clinic, Canadian Bar Association, Canadian
Association of Refugee Lawyers, Community & Legal Aid Services
Programme**
Interveners

*Registrar of Citizenship cancelling certificate of Canadian citizenship issued to
naturalized subject due to proven foreign military ties— Decision of Registrar
based on interpretation of subsection 10(b) of Bill C24— Exception stating that
naturalized Canadian Citizen accused of an offence described in section 16 or
17 of the Security of Information Act shall have citizenship status revoke.*

Citizenship Act, R.S.C. 1985, c. 29, s. 3(2)(a).
Citizenship Act, 2015. C. 24, s. 10(b)

*Appeal hearing — Whether Registrar's decision to cancel certificate of
citizenship was reasonable —*

CHAPTER SIX

Binary Trial

S was born in Iran in 1990. She first arrived in Canada on a student visa in 2010 and became a naturalized citizen on August 15, 2019. At heart, she has remained a foreign national. In reality, there is reasonable evidence to vindicate her as an agent on assignment for the Islamic Republic of Iran's intelligence service. S knowingly falsified documents to gain access into Canadian higher education institutions and actively funneled sensitive information to suspected terrorists abroad. On more than one occasion, she provided her personal credentials granting access to international scientific journals on JSTOR to friends and family members whose connections to the

Islamic Revolutionary Guards Corps is now proven. Despite her field of education in the fine arts, S's academic profiles have accessed and downloaded hundreds of thousands of articles, journals, and lab results in vastly different fields, including but not limited to nanotechnology in metallurgy, mechanics, genetics, biochemistry, astrophysics, and aerospace engineering.

Convicted of treason, S was sentenced to life imprisonment in absentia on January 20, 2020. In accordance with the verdict, the Canadian Registrar of Citizenship cancelled S's certificate based on her interpretation of s. 3(2)(a) of the Citizenship Act. This provision exempts subjects who:

a) Obtained citizenship by false representation or fraud.
b) Served as a member of an armed force or organized armed group engaged in an armed conflict with Canada.
c) Was convicted of treason, high treason, or spying offences and sentenced to imprisonment for life.
d) Was convicted of a terrorism offence or an equivalent foreign terrorism conviction and sentenced to five years of imprisonment or more.

The Registrar's decision to cancel S's certificate of citizenship was reasonable, and the Court of Appeal's decision to maintain it should be upheld. More generally, this appeal and its companion case (Canada [Attorney General], 2020 SCC 86) provide an opportunity to consider and clarify the law applicable to the judicial review of adversary deterrence.

Reasonableness review should focus on the concept of exhibiting deterrence to potential enemies of our country. Crucial deterrence is the hallmark of reasonableness review, setting it apart from the substitution of opinion permitted under correctness. Deterrence imposes three requirements on courts conducting reasonableness review. First, deterrence is the attitude that a reviewing court must adopt towards an administrative decision-maker. Deterrence mandates respect for the legislative choice to entrust a decision to certain state actors for their specialized expertise and the institutional setting in which they operate. This approach allows the legislative to put form over substance where the basis for a decision is evident on the record but does not clearly exist in written documents. As well, a court conducting deterrence review must view claims of error in context and with caution, cognizant of the need to avoid substituting its opinion for that of those empowered and better equipped to answer issues of state security and counterintelligence. By placing that perspective at the heart of the judicial review inquiry, courts must display respect for specialization and expertise, and for the legislative choice to delegate certain questions to non-judicial bodies.

[Cases Cited]
By Waine and Milena Côté, F Brown, Rowe and Martin JJ.

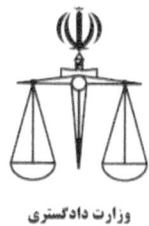

وزارت دادگستری

May 12, 2020

In the Name of God

In accordance with the request of appeal 100/19/232998, dated April 31, 2020, the fifteenth branch of the Revolutionary Court has gathered under the orders of the respectable Chief Justice to investigate the charges brought against Mrs. Khorshid Sadri (daughter of Mohammad) by the Intelligence Organization of the Islamic Revolutionary Guards Corps. Taking into consideration the court's investigations and the accused's most recent statement of defense, I hereby conclude the trial. Achieved through Allah's merciful assistance, and by relying on conscience and honor, the case details and final verdict are as follows:

Mrs. K. Sadri, born in 1990 in Isfahan, artist/

academic/gallerist, widowed, former dual citizen of Canada/Iran, has been charged with the following:

A) Espionage through acquiring classified information and provoking insurgencies

On December 21st, the anonymous soldiers of Imam al-Mahdi ambushed the accused's safehouse in Isfahan after months of scrutiny. During her arrest, multiple espionage equipment including three hard drives, two laptops, DSLR cameras, and a smartphone were confiscated. Under the auspices of the CIA and the intelligence organization of the Zionist regime, Mrs. Sadri accepted a job offer at a small art gallery in Tehran's Iranshahr district. The defendant first arose suspicion after relocating to Iran from Canada to pursue this low-paying position. Unsurprisingly, ███████████████ Gallery, in which Mrs. Sadri worked as a director, is strategically located adjacent to the local youth IRGC stronghold and a mere thirty meters from the headquarters of the Central Intelligence Ministry. During her temporary contract at the gallery, she surveilled the Iranian intelligence community's movements on an ongoing basis and actively intercepted their outgoing digital communications. As the court is aware, there exists multiple precedents in which adversary governments have conducted espionage under the guise of cultural exchange and art venues. Furthermore, the court's investigations have revealed that the defendant speaks English fluently, along with a working knowledge of Russian, Turkish, and Mandarin. She had a sequel of suspicious travel itineraries in the years prior to her arrival in Iran, some of which are listed below.

May 2018 - Armenia [simultaneous with the Velvet Revolution]
Jul 2018 - Turkey [simultaneous with increase in Kurdish militant activities against the IRGC]

████████████████████████████████

Apr 2019 - Ukraine [simultaneous with the escalations in Donetsk]
Aug 2019 - Georgia [simultaneous with that government's crackdown on IRGC's over-land sanction circumvention efforts]

B) Espionage through gathering intelligence on political affairs

The court's investigations indicate that the defendant has been collecting information on the Islamic Republic's internal and foreign affairs. Under the guise of academic research, Mrs. Sadri has taken advantage of her privileged access to unpublished archives and gradually leaked important state secrets in international journals. The titles and abstracts of her most polemical articles are as follows:

Sons of Ummah: Decolonial Warfare and the Advent of the Shia Crescent

This article is a survey of a wide array of artistic and representational trends informed by the notion of Jihad (interpreted as resistance against tyranny) as seen through the clash of western colonial forces and Iranian actors. Beginning from early Safavid illuminations portraying the conflicts over Portuguese strongholds in Hormoz and journeying all the way to the 1979 Islamic Revolution and the advent of a unique visual vocabulary geared towards attracting transnational anti-imperialist proxies, this study sheds light on the psychological dimensions of a deeply embedded nostalgia in Shia' political thought: nostalgie de la boue.

Carnation Incarnated: The Green Revolution and Its Discontents

The Portuguese Carnation Revolution was a culmination of a long struggle; so was the Iranian people's failed attempt at a revolution during the post-election protests in 2009. In the following paper, I will dissect different sociopolitical aspects of the Green Revolution and study the undercurrents that set it apart from the idyllic model of peaceful power transition imagined by the Iranian protesters. In these examinations, I will pay particular attention to parallel artistic and cultural forces that lay the foundations for both uprisings. Finally, I will investigate the lack of planetary thinking among the Iranian resistance, which in contrast to the Carnation Revolution was quickly suppressed as a localized phenomenon.

Much is Told, More is Omitted: (Un)settling Imperialism from 1974-1984

This paper focuses on unpacking a multiplicity of journalistic gazes towards the Iran-Contra Affairs: a controversial arm deal during which agents of the Israeli government trafficked weapons intended for sale to Iran through a series of clandestine networks in Lisbon. By dissecting the complicated relationship between Otelo Saraiva de Carvalho and anti-Shah religious groups in pre-revolution Iran, I will present three visual case studies in which the suspicions around the involvement of IRGC in the infamous Camarate air crash has been downplayed in western media.

C) **Actions against national security**

In her key cultural role as the gallery's director, the accused actively encouraged dissent through problematic programming. This is evident in the ministry of Islamic guidance's repeated efforts to block the contents curated by Mrs. Sadri. For example, her latest photography exhibition proposal to the ministry on November 1, 2019 set out to investigate why the municipality of Bandar Abbas demolished all but twelve columns in the city's central Sunni mosque following the ancient building's renovations in 2015 - clearly a subject chosen to provoke the Sunni minorities at a time of heightened tensions last November.

Lastly, there are dozens of documents indicting Mrs. Sadri of acquiring intelligence and reporting on martyred General Qasem Solaimani's transborder movements to adversaries. These independent corroborations are to be kept classified to ensure the safety of our beloved Quds Force troopers in Syria and Iraq.

***

Based on the aforementioned attestations, Mrs. K. Sadri's earlier convictions of high treason and actions against the national security of the holy Islamic Republic are confirmed, and the previous execution sentence handed by the third Revolutionary Court is upheld. No further appeals are accepted on this case.

[CASE CLOSED]
Court's orders were carried out on June 20, 2020 at 6:37 am.

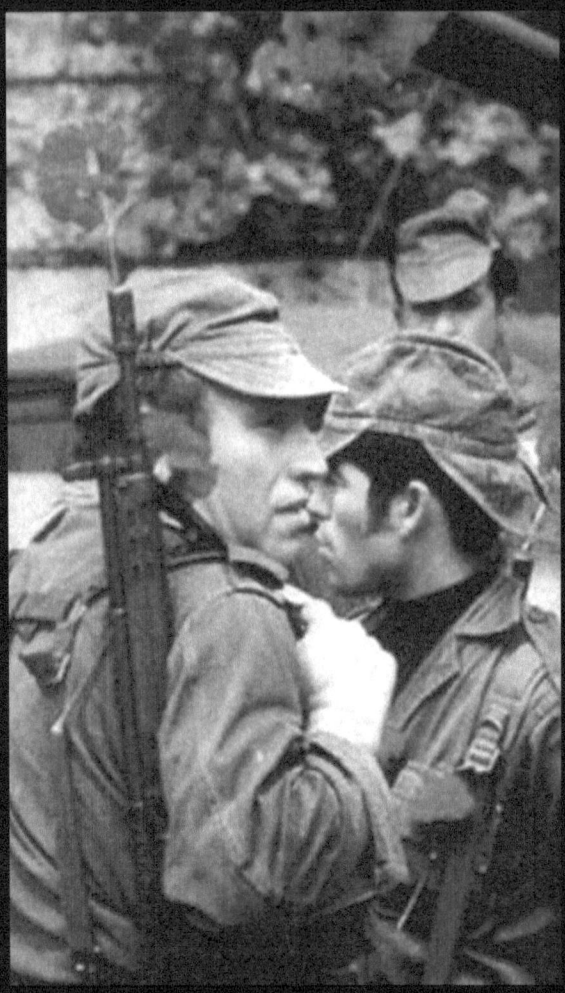

PORTUGUESE CARNATION REVOLUTION, LISBON 1974

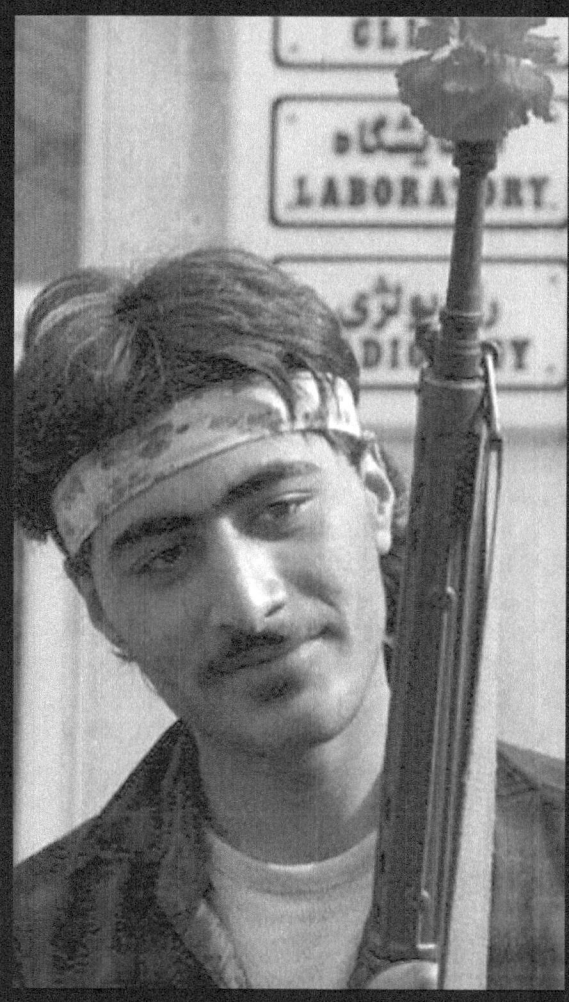

IRANIAN ISLAMIC REVOLUTION, TEHRAN 1979

ACKNOWLEDGEMENTS

This book and its accompanying exhibition wouldn't have been possible without the ongoing support, feedback and encouragement of Luisa Santos and Ana Fabíola Maurício.

I am deeply indebted to David Schnitman, my long-time friend and collaborator, for designing and materializing this book. I am grateful to Poppy Reid and Ana Marques Francisco for their keen eyes and astute feedback as my editors; and to my research assistants, Hamid Ghezloo, Dina Cheraghvand and Mohsen Ramezanzadeh whose invaluable input and collaborative spirit was central to the development of this project. I am particularly grateful to Chloé Daquet, Eurides Costa, Sara Cavaco, Schahin Paimani, Mojtaba Abu Talebi, Mohammad Reza Mokhtarian, Guy Brison and many others for their skills and kind support in the development of the accompanying exhibition. I am also thankful to Marcela Canadas, Blackwood Gallery and Hangar for their support in adapting these stories into an audiobook.

I acknowledge the generous support of the 4Cs: From Conflict to Conviviality through Creativity and Culture, a European Cooperation Project co-funded by the Creative Europe Programme of the European Union, Canada Council for the Arts, Ontario Arts Council and Toronto Arts Council in the research and development of this project. I thank the following institutions for making their archives easily accessible: Bandar Abbas Museum of Art (IR), Royal Maritime Museum (UK), Lisbon Maritime Archives (PT) and the British Library (UK).

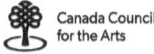 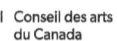 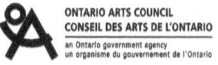

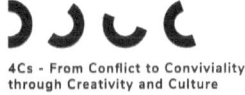 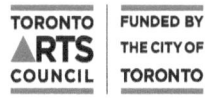

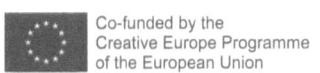